The Book of Love

The Book of Love

The Old Farmer's Almanac Reconsiders Romance, Sex, & Marriage

Christine Schultz
& the Editors of
The Old Farmer's Almanac

Villard ♕ New York

Copyright © 1996 by Yankee Publishing Inc.

Owing to limitations of space, all acknowledgments of permission to reprint previously published material and to use illustrations will be found on pages 213–14.

Schultz, Christine.
The book of love: the Old Farmer's Almanac reconsiders romance, sex and marriage / Christine Schultz and the editors of The Old Farmer's Almanac
     p. cm.
ISBN 0-679-45260-5
1. Man-woman relationships. 2. love. 3. Marriage.
4. Sexual excitement. I. Schultz, Christine. II. Old farmer's almanac. III. Title.
HQ801.S4395 1996
306.7—dc20 96-2368

Random House website address: http//www.randomhouse.com/

Printed in the United States of America on acid-free paper
98765432
First Edition

To Ray,
who knows more than
most anyone about love.

Acknowledgments

Thanks first to Sharon Smith, my editor and project manager, who had the foresight to imagine this whole project, the discipline to see it through all its stages, the wherewithal to manage a team of creative (though not always organized) players, and the cookies to congratulate me with when it was (almost) all over. Thanks also to David Rosenthal, our editor at Villard, for saying yes; Leta Evanthes and Beth Pearson at Villard for facilitating the production process; Jamie Trowbridge, director of books and new media at the Almanac, for guiding us along; John Pierce, our group publisher, for getting it going; Jud Hale, editor of the Almanac, and Susan Peery, managing editor, who first conceived and assigned to me the catalyst article for this book ("Solving the Mysteries of Love and Sex"); Dave Nelson for his good-humored design and art direction; Jill Shaffer for ever-helpful design and production guidance; J Porter for the beautiful cover design; Sarah Hale for enthusiastic and inspired art research; Jamie Kageleiry for imaginative art and editorial consultation throughout; Barbara Jatkola for meticulous copyediting and proofreading; Lori Baird for saving us from grievous errors with her careful fact checking; Nancy Trafford for her ever-cheerful assistance with all manner of manuscript details; Jacinta Monniere for keystroking; computer whiz Tom Manley for keeping us connected; Mel Allen and Tim Clark for teaching me everything I know about writing and allowing me Fridays off to write the book; Jim Collins-Laine for his good eye and kind heart as my first reader; Beffa Wyldemoon for filling out my library; Jay Heinrichs for his wonderful wit and wisdom on everything in the universe; Larry Ames, who fed me hot soup, warm love, good ideas, and support in the right combination; Diane Goodman, who lived with me through the worst of this and offered me a place to write when she could no longer live with me; all my family and friends (you know who you are), who stayed interested in the project and kept reassuring me that I would indeed finish; Mom and Dad, who provided me with the tools and the tenacity to write this book; all those — named and unnamed — whose stories appear here (especially Michael, who probably never suspected I'd tell the whole world about our first kiss); my professors at Emerson College, especially Sven Birkerts and Eileen Farrow, who approved part of this book as my master's thesis; all those individuals and institutions who helped in the field and library research — especially The Arthur and Elizabeth Schlesinger Library; the Wallace E. Mason Library at Keene State College; the Keene Public Library; the Boston Public Library; and Lorna Sagendorph Trowbridge, with her marvelous collection at the Almanac offices.

Contents

The Book of Love

An Introduction to Falling in Love

A careful look at what the scientists have learned —

and what they'll never figure out . . .

If you dropped a rock out of a 6-story (or 10- or 20-story) window 100 times and took careful note, you would be able to determine conclusively how fast that rock falls, how far, and how hard. And you would be able to predict with great accuracy what would happen the next time you dropped that rock.

But if you then dropped a man out of his everyday routine into a love affair and took careful note of how he fell that time, and the next 10 or 20 or even 100 times, you would not be able to determine with any accuracy the speed of his subsequent fall, the length of its duration, the intensity of emotion, or the mess he would be in when he hit the pavement.

For the fact is that in love the variables cannot be isolated and held constant enough to make each episode a controlled situation. Each time is different. And no matter how much we resolve to learn a lesson from lost love, there are no consistent lessons that apply. The first time the man may fall hard. The second time he may brace himself to slow his momentum and be miserable. The third time he may refuse to fall at all. The fourth, he may so dread the falling sensation that he accelerates his plummet. On the fifth fall, he may, miraculously, learn to fly.

One just does not know. Nor do the scientists, with all their charts and surveys and observations, have any more definite conclusions. But they keep trying, nonetheless. And so do we. The closer one looks at

love, the more complex the matter becomes. Perhaps its very unpredictability is the reason love remains so fascinating and worthy of study.

Now there are some who might say there's no place for science in the art of love. But that's like saying there's no place for a pooper-scooper in the joy of walking the dog. Someone's got to follow along and clean up the mess, and it might as well be the schooled observers. What the scientists can tell us about our amorous emotions may not be the whole story; certainly rising heart rates, pumping brain chemicals, and odiferous body fluids don't fully demystify the magic we feel. But they do give us concrete evidence that something is indeed taking place beyond our love-struck minds.

A Forecast for Love

If you add what the scientists know about love to what the poets know — and the historians and the animals — you're left standing just a wee bit closer to the heart of the matter. So that's what we've tried to do — take all those studies and stories concerning love and sex and romance, shake them up with a few martinis, and spill them onto the page. Our hope is that if it doesn't all make perfect scholarly sense, it might at least make a darn good book.

Our approach here is sort of like our approach to *The Old Farmer's Almanac* weather forecasts, which are prepared a full year in advance. As far as the big picture goes, we can be pretty scientific — but on a day-to-day basis, the Almanac's 80 percent accuracy rate is the best we can do. Same goes for love. We can tell you just what all the scientists say about the subject, but when it comes to the specifics of your own relationships, you have to allow for an occasional lightning strike in an unexpected place. You just never know.

As for why *The Old Farmer's Almanac* is more likely than anyone else to accurately forecast the heart's changeable climate, we've simply had more experience. For more than two centuries, the Almanac has been one of the most forthright guides to all the fundamental aspects of life — food, sex, family, love, you name it. In all that time, we've earned the reputation for being the number one source (not counting the Bible) that people turn to for guidance. Other love "authorities" have come and gone like ships in the night, but the Almanac has been faithful and enduring through the years. We're still here, still telling it like it is.

To give you a sense of what's to come, we'll say only that we've structured the book loosely along the lines of a traditional love affair — from the heart-rending search, to the thrill of first kisses, the sweetness of courtship, the excitement of engagement, the wonder of weddings, the spiced-up honeymoon, the ensuing sex-capades (well, *someone* has to wait till after matrimony these days), and finally the poignant forever after. But if you feel love is a time for wild abandon, for sampling different pleasures at different times, take heart: just because the book *appears* in that order doesn't mean you have to *read* it in that order. Love, we realize, doesn't always follow a logical path.

Nor is it something to be pursued in haste. This book, like a good love affair, will be enjoyed most if not consumed entirely in one night. Savor it little by little, picking it up again when the mood strikes. Unlike a real lover, we won't object.

With that in mind, we leave you now to begin. And we leave you, as well, to your own wild affairs, hoping that even when you cannot make scientific sense of your heart's follies, you will have learned at least to enjoy the fall: how to thrill to the sensation of air rushing past as the pavement approaches and you suddenly discover — though you're not sure how — that you've . . . *sprouted wings!* ♥

5

The
Search

If you're one of the lucky few who happened to find your sweetheart waiting like an ice cream–covered brownie at the end of the elementary school lunch line, and if you grew up to marry her and never once wondered what that cute girl across the lunchroom had in her brown paper sack, then you might want to jump right over this chapter. But if you're anything like the rest of us Almanac editors and readers who have suffered the struggles of the seemingly endless search to find that beautiful, talented, preferably rich soul mate, then maybe there's a clue here for you: a dollop of hope in the love story of the cow and the moose; a scent of success in the tale of sweat and longing; a clue to what that man has been trying to tell you when he thrusts his chest your way — it's all here in the following pages, all waiting like a fried baloney sandwich on the lunch line of love.

Love at First Smell

*One nose-wrinkling whiff may be all you need
to know if she's the one for you.*

> *As the spirits of certain people hover over music,*
> *Mine, O my love, swims upon your perfume.*
> — Charles Baudelaire, a French poet who believed
> one's soul could be found in erotic sweat

In 1986, the news hit. Scientists at Monell Chemical Senses Center in Philadelphia had proved that men's armpit odors had a pronounced effect on women. What had happened was this. For several days each week, male volunteers had worn pads discreetly tucked under their arms. The pads, moist with "male essence," were brought to scientists at the clinic, who then extracted the sweat from the pads, mixed it with alcohol, froze it, and stored it. Three times a week, unsuspecting women volunteers received a dab of the thawed essence on their upper lips. They said it smelled only of alcohol, but little did they know their lips glistened with the once-steamy musk of men. Within 12 weeks, something strange had happened. Those women with irregular menstrual cycles found that their bodies had shifted closer to the average 29.5-day cycle. The scientists took note. They had long suspected that body odors were linked with fertility matters.

At the turn of the century, medical literature had identified "The French Boarding-School Syndrome," which showed that isolation

from boys delayed puberty in girls and that young men's facial hair (a secondary sexual characteristic) grew more slowly when females were out of nose range. What's more, scientists had learned that women can detect a light sweat from about three feet away. Since a woman's sense of smell is keenest around the time of ovulation, scientists believe that smelling ability helps females select a healthy mate.

The reason smell has such a direct link to our libidos is that it moves straight from the olfactory bulbs at the roof of the nasal cavities to the limbic region of the brain. The limbic region is in charge of our

Venus, here with Adonis, follows the scent of love.

deepest emotions — fear, rage, hate, ecstasy, lust — and smells have a direct dial to that hot spot. They needn't check through the neocortex — the switching station of the thinking brain — as sight and sound must do. What we get from odors, therefore, is pure sensory impression: peppermint, pears, rotten eggs. Damage to the limbic area can diminish memory and the libido, but if all is working as it should, we have 5 million olfactory neurons to detect more than 10,000 odors. With each aroma come associations that can conjure up a complete memory many years later. The perfume of a stranger on the street can arouse a mood of unfounded intimacy. *(Do I know you?)*

Because sweat is one of the most subliminally arousing perfumes of all, people in countries around the world have long made it the active ingredient of love potions. During festivals in Greece and the Balkans, men still tuck handkerchiefs in their armpits, then present them to women as an invitation to dance. Likewise, the women of Shakespeare's day saturated peeled apples with underarm odors and presented them to lovers as smelly treats. In the Caribbean, hamburger patties steeped in sweat are cooked and served to the woman or man of one's dreams.

The Sordid Underside

But as everyone knows, body odor can be just as repelling when sweet sweat goes sour. Although pure sweat isolated in a lab remains odorless for at least two weeks, sweat on the body can stink within six hours. The culprit is bacteria. It lurks in underarm crevices. Armpit hair adds surface area and radiates odor molecules into the air like college students charging to Daytona on spring break. Some are smellier than others, but everyone's body odor stems from the same place — the apocrine glands.

Apocrine glands, located around the armpits, face, chest, genitals, and anus, are activated by sex hormones during puberty. Other glands, called the eccrine glands, provide a cooling system. As much as three gallons of sweat can

Mum worked on sweat as well as on the psyche of American consumers. To perspire was a social disgrace.

pour from the eccrine glands in 24 hours — which is all well and good for the scientists at Monell, but not so great for the dripping young suitor. What's a smitten boy to do?

For five millennia, people have worked to stem the tide of perspiration. The Egyptians tried scented baths, perfumed underarm oils, and removal of armpit hair. The Greeks and Romans resorted to masking their body odors with perfume. But none of the great thinkers of ancient times could effectively cork the moisture of humankind.

Then, at last, came Mum. Introduced in 1888, Mum used a zinc compound in a cream base and worked not only on sweat but also on the psyches of American consumers. To create a market, the promoters of the first antiperspirant raised concerns about women's "daintiness" and "sweetness." The cause of the trouble was never directly mentioned, but women caught on; they no longer had an excuse for unsightly underarm stains. Mum was the word.

The market grew. In 1902, there were consumers enough to push a second antiperspirant onto the market. This one, called Everdry, included an extra drying ingredient. In 1908 a third, labeled Hush, joined in. The name was perfect; in drugstores everywhere, embarrassed Americans requested the product in the same whispered tone they used to select a prophylactic.

To perspire was a social disgrace — but one not to be mentioned in national magazines until the bold debut of Odo-Ro-No in 1914. Odo-Ro-No promoters shocked turn-of-the-century sensibilities by challenging consumers to take the true "Armhole Odor Test" — a hearty sniff to the blouse. The cause of that smell, proclaimed advertisers, now had a name. They called the culprit "B.O."

Masking Our Desire

The word was out, and anyone who wasn't underarmed with deodorant wasn't safe. In the 1930s, advertisers expanded their target to include men. Deodorant became as essential as soap. It sold by the ton. But in all the rush to become fragrantly civilized, people neglected one important fact: the body odors they sought to mask were the very

I Will Smell You From Afar, My Love

Flaubert is said to have kept his lover's slippers and mittens in his desk drawer so that in her absence, he could luxuriate in her bouquet.

11

scents that had been the most stirring.

Something had become obscured in the deodorizing process — something randy and raucous. From men to mice, sex lay in the scents. Not only could the smell of male mouse urine make the uterus of a female mouse grow heavy in a matter of minutes, but the whiff of female mouse urine could make a male mouse sprout to maturity.

Animal magnetism lay in the body's secretions; they could draw mates from afar. Nearly a century ago, French entomologist Jean-Henri Fabre saw what one newly metamorphosed female moth could do to a male. He had left the fluttering creature caged in the study of his country home overnight. In the morning, he found that 40 male moths from the neighborhood had entered through the open window. Within a few more days, more than 150 males had arrived in a frenzy of passion, some coming from as far as seven miles away.

Other scientists saw it, too. One dab of methyl p-hydroxybenzoate (an arousing chemical compound) on a female dog not in estrus, and all the male dogs in the neighborhood showed up with tails wagging.

Next time she says, "Honey, you're such a boar!" take it as a compliment.

White-tailed deer went for males that reeked of urine. Female lemmings chose mates that defeated other males and still smelled of victory a whole day later.

Perfect Scents

Whether we like it or not, our own predeodorant bodies send off messages of attraction, like billboards flashing at a busy intersection. Excitement and stress cause more cholesterol excretions. Those in turn convert to sex hormones — progesterone, testosterone, androsterone. Androsterone is a great stimulant — just a dab of it drew laboratory subjects unknowingly to certain seats in an empty theater. (Interestingly enough, it's also the active ingredient in Boar Mate, a sex stimulant for sows.)

The Odds of Finding Your True Love in Alaska

In Alaska, where women are outnumbered by men about 10 to 1 (and by sled dogs by about 20 to 1), they have a saying about finding a man: "The odds are good, but the goods are odd."

In fact, most perfumes we wear are based on the sexual secretions of animals — cats, deer, and whales. The scent of the European wild boar also is popular, because it most closely resembles — wouldn't you know it — men's sweat. "The fecal odor of straight civet would turn one's stomach," writes Diane Ackerman in *A Natural History of the Senses,* "but in small doses it converts perfume into an aphrodisiac." Smells shock and fascinate us; that's why we like them, says a perfume maker who sniffs up to a hundred fragrances a day: "Our lives are quiet. We like to be disturbed by delight." In fact, a survey by the Fragrance Foundation shows that women and men rank scent at 8.4 on a scale of 1 to 10 for what's arousing in the opposite sex. Maybe that's why some people will pay $300 an ounce for a bottle of Pheromone, which, according to its name, should smell like what our own bodies produce — for free.

Every year Americans spend a billion and a half dollars on fragrances and even more on deodorants — great sums of money to mask our animalistic odors, and great sums more to re-create them when, ironically, a drop of a man's sweat on the upper lip would have done just as well. All we can hope is that when all is said and done, it comes out making perfect scents. ♥

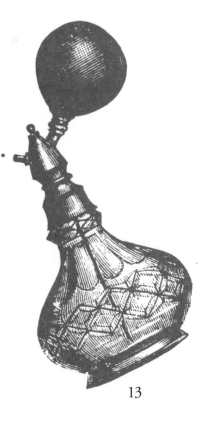

13

Of Moose & Men: The Odd Couple of the Animal Kingdom

Herewith, an unbelievable — but true — eight-legged story that could happen to two-legged you.

This story, like many love stories, involves a male, a female, sex, a (near) wedding, broken hearts, and longing. But this is not an ordinary love story, for the virile male in this tale is a moose and the sweet-faced female a Hereford. And though their love was never meant to be, it miraculously came to pass.

It was a quiet October morning in 1986, high in the hills of Shrewsbury, Vermont. A moose, later named Josh, emerged from the woods with his eyes fixed on a brown-and-white Hereford called Jessica. She mooed loudly, as did her cow companions, for they had never seen a bull moose like Josh. He stood six feet at the shoulders, a brownish black bulk on slender legs with a broad, pendulous nose. His two-foot-high antlers were distinctive; on each side, five points were cupped toward the sky, and one in front was angled oddly downward. Even from a distance, it gave Josh a rakish look — made him seem different.

And maybe Josh *was* different, for that evening he made a

When Josh set his heart on Jessica, the result was a love affair that even wildlife experts couldn't explain.

How to Flirt with a Firefly

Hold a small flashlight close to the ground. Watch for the flash of a flying firefly. Count two seconds (one thousand one, one thousand two) and flick on your flashlight for one second. (This mimics the code the female firefly uses to lure the male.) The firefly will turn and come toward you. Continue flashing for love. The firefly will soon light on your hand. What happens next is none of our business.

☞ From The ☜ Old Farmer's Almanac

Folklore has it that if a young woman sees a dove and glimpses the new Moon at the same instant, she should repeat: "Bright Moon, clear Moon, Bright and fair, Lift up your right foot, There'll be a hair." When she removes her shoe, she'll find a hair the color of her future husband's.

—1994

break from the mostly solitary life of an *Alces alces* and plunged into the society of the three dairy cows. At his approach, one cow and her yearling bolted through the electric fence. Jessica, the plump Hereford with a splash of freckles across her nose, stood her ground. She watched the tall, dark stranger as he circled — moving ever closer — until he had come within a few feet, then she coyly stepped away. Josh persisted. As the light faded to black, the mismatched pair stood silhouetted in the field, side by side.

The next day found Josh still in pursuit of the lovely bovine. By late morning, he'd earned nuzzling privileges. He caressed her back with his chin while she ate. The intimacy made him bold, and he boosted his 700-pound frame briefly upon hers. But that's where Jessica drew the line and backed off. She'd been through this before with a white-faced bull and had borne two calves. Josh, by comparison, was a novice. He was a two-and-a-half-year-old teenager inept in mating matters, and Jessica was not impressed. So it seemed the initial attraction of opposites should end right there — but Josh would not budge from his sweetheart's side. He lay five feet from her, chewing his cud as she chewed hers. They stared into each other's eyes.

As the weeks passed and Josh did not, word spread through town. The media arrived in full force and buzzed the news across the country, then overseas. Thousands of people, hearing the reports, found their way to the village of 600, then up the dirt road to the pasture where the moose courted the farmer's cow. There they looked and shook their heads, smiled and made comments.

"Jessica looks kind of confused," said one.

"Everyone in love looks confused," replied Larry Carrara, the farmer who owned Jessica.

Before long, folks down in Nashville had capitalized on the affair. They pressed a country-and-western single called "The Lovesick Moose," which became a national hit. Two other companies followed suit with ballads about the odd couple. It was all so sweet and silly that even the musicians laughed during the recording:

She was such a lady,
in his eyes she looked so fine.
But it weren't her chromosomes
that were on his mind.

Had her chromosomes, in fact, been on Josh's mind, he would have realized he hadn't a chance. They had inherited genes from different breeds. Jessica bore the legacy of the Bovidae family (a distant relative to buffalo and sheep), while Josh belonged to the Cervidaes, cousins to the common deer. Theirs was the *West Side Story* of the wild kingdom.

The Key to Mating Matters

As early as 1914, Frank Rattray Lillie at the University of Chicago had shown that all animals — whether moose or mouse — are bound by the "lock-and-key" hypothesis. In other words, each egg has receptors that recognize only sperm of its own species, like a lock knows a key. Of course, there are exceptions — like the male donkey who mates with the female horse to make a mule. Or the female donkey who couples with the male horse to make a hinny. But neither a mule nor a hinny can make a thing, so what's the evolutionary point to that? It's the reproductive road to ruin.

A fact of life that should have made Josh take one look at Jessica and decide, "I wouldn't mate with you if you were the last ungulate on earth." But, says nature writer Sy Montgomery, "it's a matter of individual taste. Everyone knows someone who's going out with some guy who's such bad news you want to set his hair on fire. Animals do that, too."

The "lock-and-key" theory says this is unlikely.

17

Although he had failed to consummate the relationship, Josh stayed on at the Carraras' farm. He continued to lie beside Jessica through the first month, then the second, and into the third. Local wildlife experts couldn't explain it and gave up trying to predict when the lovesick moose would leave.

One Endless Season of Longing

Had Josh been the average moose with the average sexual preference, he could easily have found fulfillment among his own. In the worst-case scenario, he'd have had to wait 10 days for a female moose to come into estrus (the time that humans would have used to get to know each other better — where they'd gone to school, what flavor ice cream they preferred, and all that seductive stuff). Then, after mating, he'd still have had plenty of time during the two-month rut to find (by bugling out a sort of moose singles ad) and copulate with another female moose or two. Three quick sexual flings could have been his, but he chose instead one endless season of longing.

Could it be that Josh was the only moose ever to act that way? No, said the folks at several wildlife departments, it had happened before. Each fall a couple of calls reporting similar cases had come to their offices. In the Adirondacks, there were reports of a 1,300-pound moose, nicknamed Big Richard, who appeared several years in a row in mid-September at area farms. The dairy cows rebuffed his attentions, and the horses acted high-strung, but in 1988 a yearling pig named May Dawn returned Big Richard's affections. "He seems to have taken up quite an attachment with the pig, and the pig with Big Richard," farmer Fred Winderl of Saranac Lake said at the time. "If they're compatible, it's all right with me. I'm just waiting to see what develops." Nothing ever did, according to Ken Kogut, manager of the Bureau of Environmental Protection at the New York Department of Environmental Conservation. For the record, Kogut would like to clarify the relationship. "Big Richard didn't try to do the act with the pig," Kogut insists. "They were just friends."

In other years, there were other calls about overzealous moose chasing heifers around barnyards. Environmental enforcement officer Donald Gallus of Mount Holly, Vermont, remembers one episode in 1976 that locals talk about still. A 900-pound moose had been stalking a Morrisville dairy farm, threatening anyone who tried to milk the cows. State game wardens attempted to tranquilize the moose and haul it to a wildlife sanctuary near the Canadian border, but the moose escaped and kidnapped a herd of heifers from a dairy farm in nearby Holland. When two men discovered the moose guarding the bovine hostages, the angry creature chased the men up a tree.

Moose, of course, have no herding instinct, so perhaps it was the rush of hormones in autumn that made that moose and others like him a little crazy. Another case in point occurred more recently in Waterboro, Maine. A 700-pound moose, enamored of a foam deer, mounted the object of his affection. Caught in the emotion of the moment, the moose was oblivious to the fact that he had jounced the antlers off his inanimate partner. Only when the deer's whole head tumbled to the ground in the head-over-heels affair did the moose dismount and look around. He took a sniff, and another look, then trotted into the woods.

Such incidents, it would seem, should occur more frequently in places where the moose population is thin, leaving the male moose more desperate for companionship. But the Waterboro moose lives in a state with 25,000 others — more of his kind than in any other state except Alaska. And, in fact, whether there are 20 moose in the state (such as in New York) or 5,000 (in New Hampshire), wildlife biologists receive roughly the same number of calls. Moose biologist Kristine Bontaites of New Hampshire's Fish and Game Department says that's because a moose's sexual preference has less to do with the size of the herd than with the age of the individual. Every year, she explains, young bulls come into rut from late September through November (sort of like what happens to teenage boys in spring). And although they're capable of reproducing

when they're as young as a year and a half, they aren't allowed to breed with a cow moose until they've fully matured (not unlike women who flirt with the novice but become engaged to the expert). "For a couple of years, they're young, horny teenagers with no place to go," says Bontaites. "The moose cows say, 'Hey, Junior, you don't know what you're doing,' and will rear up and strike the young bull with their hoofs. After treatment like that, the young bulls just keep moving until they find a female who doesn't protest — any four-legged animal that can't run away will do."

So it was that Josh had set his heart on Jessica. He continued to stand by her and tried his best to impress her. He'd puff his upper lip, flare his nostrils, and blow through vibrating lips. He'd urinate, kneel to sniff his own musk, and then toss his head and bugle. Jessica wasn't always interested. One time, when she'd had enough, she snuck under a pine tree with branches too low for Josh to pass under, and stood out of reach. He waited, gazing at her from a few feet away. Finally she emerged, lumbered toward him, and, as if by way of apology, rubbed her head on his shoulder. Josh seemed pleased. He pushed hay toward her with his muzzle. While she ate, he laid his head on her back. He wasn't hungry for the cattle feed himself; he just wanted to make sure that Jessica got more than the others.

We Are Gathered Here Together . . .

It was all so dear that eventually some 75,000 spectators came to see the barnyard romance for themselves. They bought T-shirts, bumper stickers, and other souvenirs bearing the odd couple's image. The farmer, Larry Carrara, could hardly keep up with the orders. He took a leave of absence from his job. He wanted to make sure that Jessica and Josh weren't bothered by the onlookers, who took pictures, took notes, and couldn't help but take the odd couple to heart.

For the most part, there weren't any problems. But then one Saturday, a state representative came unasked to consecrate the courtship by marrying the cow and moose before 4,000 witnesses. As an official justice of the peace, the representative had the power to perform the wedding, but what he didn't have was a signature from the cow or moose on the marriage certificate. Nor did he have the farmer's approval. "I think this has gone far enough," Larry Carrara said. "I don't want a sideshow here."

And so the couple's love remained illicit — which made no difference, of course, to Josh and Jessica. What mattered to them was their time together. For 75 days, they kept company, sharing a bond deeper than any other dairy cow and moose had ever shared. It seemed their relationship might go on forever. But then, just as quickly as the affair had begun, something snapped between them. More specifically, something snapped off Josh.

On the morning of November 25, an antler lay on the ground. The next day, the other fell off as well, and where there had once been two mighty appendages, now there was only a pair of unsightly sores. Josh looked naked. He looked embarrassed. As Larry put it, Josh had lost his "mooseculinity." The next day, Josh was gone. Jessica stayed in the barnyard. She looked in all directions. She saw no sign of her mighty moose.

In the decade since, Josh has returned to the farm only once, the following fall. The horses scared him away. There is no way of knowing whether the lovesick moose ever fell in love with another cow. Nor can we know for certain whether Jessica quit watching for the tall, dark stranger to return. The only thing we can be sure of is that, for a time, two mismatched creatures stayed side by side against all odds. And that their remarkable affection inspired tens of thousands to leave their daily routines and come see for themselves what had taken place. Of those who witnessed the affair, some concluded that it was based purely on lust. But many more insisted it had been love. They'd seen with their own eyes proof that opposites could attract and stay together in the animal kingdom — at least for a time. And seeing that had confirmed their hope that maybe, just maybe, it could happen to them. ♥

Looking for Love
at a Country Dance

Pay close attention to how she walks,

how she talks, and how she bares her teeth.

The Peterborough,
New Hampshire, Town Hall suited our purposes well, for a balcony at the back allowed us to see the entire room at a glance and to take notes on the contradancers below without their knowing. My three colleagues and I had come to watch for courtship signals — the Primate Crotch Display, the Sequential Flirting Gesture, and the Copulatory Gaze — which had been outlined by social scientists in earlier studies. We wished to see for ourselves whether singles would exhibit such courtship behavior under natural conditions. Tonight the town hall would be our lab.

To ensure a thorough investigation, my colleagues and I agreed to circulate among the participants and return periodically to record our observations in a notebook at the upper station. We kept the notebook concealed and filed our reports under code

Sociologists and singles alike will recognize the baring of the teeth as the "Nervous Social Smile."

To the scientific observer, the dance hall becomes a pulsating laboratory of love.

names so as not to risk detection. We had also taken care to dress as the participants did, wearing loose cotton clothing. Such precautions in dress and manner, we hoped, would keep our subjects from becoming inhibited while we monitored their every move.

The Laboratory of Love

Observation began at 8 P.M. Our subjects entered the room along the hall's edges, establishing territorial boundaries by marking chairs with their belongings. Most women kept their coats on and maintained closed body postures. Their iciness, we feared, would slow the social proceedings. Women, according to sociologist Timothy Perper's bar study, initiate 85 percent of heterosexual encounters. They do this by drawing attention to themselves: arching backs, swaying hips, fluffing hair.

Darwin would approve of males who subconsciously seek out a 1:1.3 waist-to-hip ratio — a cue to better health and fertility.

The men, meanwhile, stood with legs spread, hands on hips, or sat with legs wide — demonstrating what zoologist Desmond Morris calls "The Primate Crotch Display." Others rolled their shoulders, stretched, or puffed their chests. They were watching and being watched. The looking "eye to body" stage of Morris's Sexual Sequence had begun.

What they were subconsciously looking for, according to Steven Gangestad and Randy Thornhill of the University of New Mexico, was a partner with an average face — one that approached symmetry. Symmetry, it seems, highlights those closest to the genetic average and suggests that they're resistant to disease. Likewise, a clear complexion reflects health, so cultures worldwide consider good skin attractive. The other feature most men subconsciously seek out is a satisfying hip-to-waist ratio. In a recent paper, Devendra Singh of the University of Texas showed that men were more attracted to women whose hips were roughly one-third larger than their waists. The theory goes that a woman who stores fat on her hips rather than her waist tends toward higher fertility and lower disease. Whether that's true or not, the proportion has been so pleasing that it hasn't changed for the winning Miss America in the past few decades despite the fact that the winners now are 30 percent slimmer than those in the past.

So it was that our subjects eyed each other, sizing up potential mates (or dance partners, at least). In the rear corner — what some dancers call the "pickup alley" — a white-haired man approached

The caller speeds the intimacy, acting as a minister of love. Standing elevated on-stage, he wields the microphone as his staff, with the power of the fiddle and banjo flowing through him to the dancers.

a young female. She crossed her arms in what Desmond Morris calls "The Body-cross": a classic "barrier signal . . . forming a temporary 'bar' across the trunk, rather like a bumper or fender on the front of a motor car." The white-haired man missed the young woman's cue and asked her to dance. She avoided eye contact and shook her head from extreme left to right. Her lips lifted over her upper and lower teeth, and we made note of the snarl. "The Nervous Social Smile," writes Helen Fisher in *The Anatomy of Love,* "plays a distinctly negative role in courtship. It stems from the ancient mammalian practice to bare one's teeth when cornered."

At last, the older gentleman realized his error and hurried off. The young woman spotted an attractive young man with good skin. She shifted her posture: her head tilted slightly, her shoulders lifted, and her feet rotated to the pigeon-toed position. This, we noted, was "The Meekness Cue," the female signal permitting the male to come closer. Their eyes met in what Morris terms "The Mutual Gaze Condition." The young man approached and requested a dance. She nodded, and he reached for her hand to lead her to the dance floor. As Morris suggests, this initial touching stage is often disguised as directional guidance. First contact increases intimacy, with nerve endings speeding exciting messages to the brain.

Love Lyrics to Die For

Sooner or later, everyone realizes that country-and-western music is all about unrequited love — full of angst and emotion. But what about the poor soul who has to listen to the stuff after having just lost his best girl? Sociologist Jim Gundlach of Alabama's Auburn University wanted to test his hunch that the idea of "single men lined up at the country music bar drinking their beer as the music wails about being alone" was not a healthy one. He plotted the suicide rates for 49 major metropolitan areas against the radio time devoted by each to country music. Sure enough, he found the greater the country music airplay, the higher the suicide rate.

So far, so good. But if the courtship sequence doesn't continue to progress at a pace comfortable to both partners, one will break it off. Caution during courtship is key. Helen Fisher compares it to spider interplay: "The male wolf spider must enter the long, dark entrance of a female's compound in order to court and copulate. This he does slowly. If he is overeager, she devours him."

The Fevered Dance

The stakes were high as our subjects prepared to dance. The woman stood parallel to all the other women, the man shoulder to shoulder with the other men. The couple's eyes lingered on each other. Each took in the contours of the other's face, looking most often at the eyes and mouth. Voice-to-voice contact would determine next whether courtship continued. If no common interests or values were found, intrigue would drop.

From where we sat, it didn't look good. The woman, having nothing to say, stared over the man's shoulder, scoping the three other lines of men facing women. She glanced out the large windows to the full moon, looked up toward the balcony (failed to detect us!), and then rested her view on the four musicians on-stage waiting for the caller's direction.

Things move along quickly when the dance calls for a waist embrace.

"Has everyone found a partner?" the caller asked. He surveyed the room. "Touch your partner," he teased. "Grab hold of your partner." The young woman reached toward the clear-skinned man, obeying the caller's cue with an arm-to-shoulder embrace. Under normal conditions, the Sexual Sequence would not have progressed so quickly, but, as Morris notes, "an invitation to dance can bring a waist embrace forward to an early stage in courtship." The caller speeded the intimacy, acting as a minister of love. Standing elevated on-stage, he wielded the microphone as his staff, with the power of the fiddle and banjo flowing through him to the dancers.

"Take hands four from the top," he called. Hands reached out uniting men and women. Sets of four formed, with the pair facing away from the stage becoming "active." The active couples would turn and twirl their way toward the back of the hall, while the "inactive" pairs would mostly watch and wait for their turn to frolic as they moved up the line toward the stage.

Cues to the Chaos of Courtship

The fiddle jumped, the piano pounded, and the pulse pushed through the hall. A latent charge of neurochemicals kicked in. "Active couples balance and swing your partners," the caller shouted. The couples kicked back from each other, then pulled together. They swung with abandon. For eight long beats, the dancers stared into their partners' eyes. All else faded into the background, like laundry spinning in the dryer.

Unknowingly, our subjects checked each other's pupils for dilation. Enlarged pupils reveal pleasure and excitement, making the looker more attractive to the lookee. "The more her pupils expand with emotional excitement," writes Morris, "the more it makes his expand, and vice versa." But the caller's voice interrupted the arousing glances. "Ladies' chain across," he said. Women reluctantly abandoned their men, crossed by other women, and ended facing new men. "Courtesy turn the ladies," the caller said, directing each gentleman to slip his arm around the waist of an unfamiliar female. In most cases, two strangers were now in full body contact, with hands close to sexual regions. Under standard social conditions, many might resist, but the dance's stylized flirtations made it safe and fun. Singles flirted wantonly. Anything went, as long as they heeded the caller's cues. "Ladies," he shouted, "chain back home to your partner — he's waiting there for you."

The reunited couples had then progressed one

The Odds Against Classified Love

According to Masters and Johnson, the average number of responses a woman will get from placing a personal ad in the newspaper is 49. For men, only 15.

A grown-up version of "London Bridge"? Not quite.
Instead, these two may be falling for each other.

place down the line. Now the next pair repeated the sequence. Among the whirling skirts and touching hands, we noted prolonged eye contact and heads tilting seductively at strangers. From the balcony, we watched the two lines of men and women blend and twist together like DNA molecules exchanging genetic patterns. The formalized steps offered order to the otherwise chaotic mystery of courtship.

The Decisive Moment

"Long lines forward and back," the caller said. A line of women with their arms around each other's waists moved toward a line of similarly positioned men. The opposite sexes nodded at each other, almost brushing noses. Among the crowd, we spotted a blond woman making a special courtship display. She opened her eyes wide at a man in glasses; lifted her eyebrows in a swift, jerky motion; dropped her eyelids; tilted her head down and to the side; and looked away. A textbook example of what German ethologist Irenaus Eibl-Eibesfeldt has labeled "The Sequential Flirting Gesture." Such an elaborate series of movements is hard to imagine until you see it in action. Eibl-Eibesfeldt contends it's an innate courtship ploy that women worldwide evolved eons ago to signal sexual interest.

With a final note, the music stopped, leaving our subjects in a sweat. The last of the coats and inhibitions had been discarded. Taking advantage of the energetic mood, the caller said, "One of the traditions of contradancing is to swap partners." The dancers moved to obey, each searching for a new mate.

The dance began again amid a pungent smell that had developed in the hall. The vigorous movement had stirred primordial scent glands into action, and the wash of smells unhinged the dancers. Passionate stomping and whooping indicated that the ritual was at full tilt. The hour had passed eleven, but our subjects seemed not to notice. Neurochemicals were at work. During the early stages of infatuation, the brain releases the chemical phenylethylamine (PEA), which acts like an amphetamine. When mice are injected with PEA, they jump and squeal, exhibiting what scientists call "popcorn behavior." In an effort to channel that wild emotion, the caller announced a waltz. It was the last dance. All night dancers had gladly traded partners in search of the perfect mate; now the moment of final selection had arrived.

The key prize in this round, it seemed, was the caller himself. His reputation for courtly love reached down the eastern seaboard. For several years, he had played the game of Musical Mates with such grace that women had repeatedly sought him out. He had found himself overwhelmed by his own statistics. The right woman could change all that — make him monogamous.

And there she was, waiting at the foot of the stage. He descended to her with a smile, and placed a firm hand on her back. The fiddle music encircled them, and they spun with confidence around the hall. They smiled without baring teeth. His eyes locked deep into hers.

We took note of the signal specified by Helen Fisher: during the Copulatory Gaze, "men and women often stare intently at a potential mate for about two or three seconds during which their pupils may dilate." This, Fisher explained, stimulates in the other party a fight or flight response.

The Final Waltz

But it seemed to us then that neither the caller nor his partner had either fight or flight in mind. They stepped together. Twirled. Two bodies as one. A classic case, Timothy Perper would note, of full-body synchronization. "Finally, they are looking at each other nearly continuously, touching each other regularly, talking face-to-face and moving in full-body synchrony with each other," Perper explains. "Generally, in a public place, intimacy does not increase further, though sometimes the couple will start to kiss each other."

And sure enough, they did. Desmond Morris calls the kiss "the first seriously arousing intimacy" and says it can lead to other things. Our subjects tonight stopped short of that. Their lips parted, and they continued to waltz around the hall. Her thin, dark braid flew free, but her forehead pressed close to his. "This is an excluding action," writes Morris, "cutting the rest of us off from the pair." Obviously no longer welcome, we took that as our cue to leave. ♥

Fifteen Pickup Lines Guaranteed to Lose with the Ladies

In his study of opening lines used by men to meet women, psychologist Chris Kleinke came upon the following 15 openers that nice guys will want to avoid:

In general situations

1. Is that really your hair?
2. You remind me of a woman I used to date.
3. Your place or mine?

In bars

4. (Looking at a woman's jewelry): Wow, it looks like you just robbed Woolworth's.
5. Bet I can outdrink you.
6. I play the field, and I think I just hit a home run with you.
7. Do you think I deserve a break today?
8. I bet the cherries jubilee isn't as sweet as you are.
9. If this food doesn't kill us, the bill will.

In supermarkets

10. Do you really eat that junk?
11. You shouldn't buy that. It's full of cholesterol.
12. Is your bread fresh?

In Laundromats

13. A man shouldn't have to wash his own clothes.
14. Those are some nice undies you have there.
15. I'll wash your clothes if you'll wash mine.

The Kiss

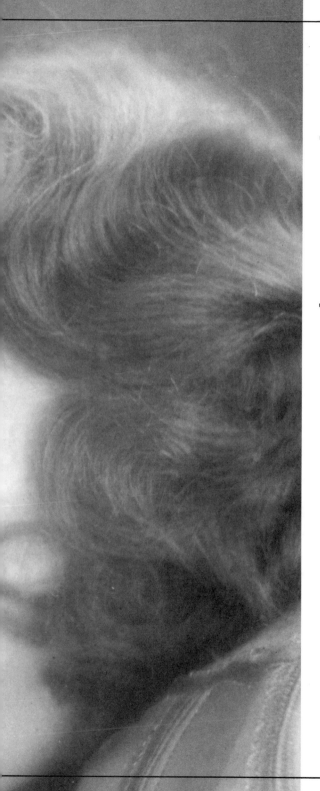

Kisses.

You can read about them all you want — first kisses, screen kisses, talking kisses, electric kisses. If you are a serious student of kissing, you can even memorize the whole glossary of kissing terms provided in the following pages. But, to be perfectly truthful, the best way we at *The Old Farmer's Almanac* have found to do our (purely scientific) research on the subject is to drive with a handsome lab partner to a scenic overlook and proceed to examine the species and family and phylum of kissing in as much depth and in as many variations and combinations as possible in the time available. We recommend you do the same.

The Science of Osculation

Nothing to it, you think, but there are a few things about kissing you might not know...

*I kissed my first woman and smoked my first cigarette on the same day.
I have never had time for tobacco since.*
— Arturo Toscanini

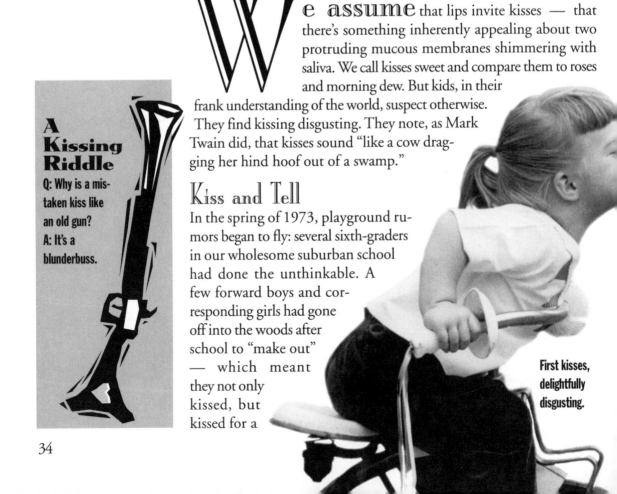

We **assume** that lips invite kisses — that there's something inherently appealing about two protruding mucous membranes shimmering with saliva. We call kisses sweet and compare them to roses and morning dew. But kids, in their frank understanding of the world, suspect otherwise. They find kissing disgusting. They note, as Mark Twain did, that kisses sound "like a cow dragging her hind hoof out of a swamp."

Kiss and Tell

In the spring of 1973, playground rumors began to fly: several sixth-graders in our wholesome suburban school had done the unthinkable. A few forward boys and corresponding girls had gone off into the woods after school to "make out" — which meant they not only kissed, but kissed for a

First kisses, delightfully disgusting.

A Kissing Riddle
Q: Why is a mistaken kiss like an old gun?
A: It's a blunderbuss.

34

long time. We fifth-grade girls were appalled. Late one night at a slumber party, we resolved that if we had to kiss in order to grow up, we'd at least hold out till high school. High school seemed far off still, and we hoped by then to have figured a way out of kissing (as we'd managed to slip out of doing the dishes). The problem was that boys our age actually liked (or pretended to like) all things slimy, and when they heard about saliva sharing (Really?! How gross! Let's try it!), their eyes lit up. Unfortunately, they needed partners — and that meant us.

Throughout the summer of '73, Michael and Paul tried hard to persuade my friend Diane and me to make out with them. Being too embarrassed to approach each of us directly, Paul asked me if I would make out with Michael, and Michael asked Diane if she would make out with Paul.

"No way," I said.

"We're too young," she said.

But that fall, after we'd entered sixth grade and our exalted status as the oldest kids at school had settled upon us, we became emboldened. Maybe just one kiss, we conceded, to confirm how positively disgusting it was. I told Paul to tell Michael I'd meet him at the big log in the woods, at four o'clock, on Friday.

On Friday, I couldn't concentrate. All through social studies, I considered backing out. During the break before math, I tried to find Paul to tell Michael to scratch the plan. No luck. The last bell blasted. It was up to me to meet Michael at the log and tell him myself.

Michael arrived wearing Levi cords, as most boys did then, with a T-shirt tucked in at the waist and his hands tucked in at the pockets. He was grinning. His ears stuck out. In first grade, he had chased me around the playground and I'd affectionately kicked him in the shins. In second

The Definition of Deceit

When Noah Webster, author of America's first dictionary, was caught kissing the chambermaid, his wife is reported to have said, "Why, Noah, I'm surprised!"

To which he supposedly replied, "Madam, *you* are astonished; *I* am surprised."

Chimps do it, too, but they just don't have the range.

grade, he'd written me penciled love letters wadded into squares. In third and fourth grades, he'd ignored me completely (or so I thought until Diane pointed out that he hit the ball harder when I was around). But all that had been when we were young. Now things had matured between us — we were eleven. He climbed onto the log and sat about four feet away.

"Hi," he said.

"Hi," I said back.

Having exhausted the extent of our intimate conversation, we passed the next 10 minutes in silence. I thought desperately of ways to tell him I'd chickened out, while he thought desperately of ways to get me closer.

"Look," he finally said, "I'll count down from ten, and at one we'll kiss. Okay?"

It sounded stupid. "Sure," I said, stalling for time.

He began to count. Ten . . . nine . . . eight . . . I began to sweat. It occurred to me then that there was a lot I didn't know about kissing.

The Anatomy of a Kiss

"Now, of course, it is quite clear that one of the first requisites for a kiss is a mouth," wrote Dr. Christopher Nyrop, professor of romance philology, in his 1901 account, *The Kiss and Its History*. "A kiss is produced by a kind of sucking movement of the muscles of the lips, accompanied by a weaker or louder sound. . . . This movement of the muscles, however, is not of itself sufficient to produce a kiss, it being, as you know, employed by coachmen when they want to start their horses; but it becomes a kiss only when it is used as an expression of a certain feeling, and when the lips are pressed against, or simply come in contact with, a living creature or object."

Human lips can so simply come in contact with living creatures because evolution has turned them inside out. Of all the primates, man is the only species with "conspicuously everted lips," according to zoologist Desmond Morris. Although chimpanzees and other animals use kisses to communicate, they lack the range of flexibility we humans have.

That flexibility so intrigued plastic surgeons at Queen Victoria's Hospital in England that they made a body scanner movie of lip muscles in action. It was the first such movie ever made, and they learned a lot. We work 20 muscles to form a kiss, they found, including the strong orbicularis oris muscle, which encircles the lips. And when people kiss, the surgeons noted, they shift mouth positions often. The surgeons said that people do this because facial muscles fatigue quickly. They didn't say it might just be more fun.

Lips are amazing. When sexually aroused, they swell and redden, mimicking the labia. Women fake a heightened sexual state by applying a coat of lipstick or gloss, which in our culture makes them more attractive. In many non-Western cultures, fat, red lips are shocking, and even uncolored faces are covered with veils.

Kissing Concerns

The fact is that lips are the only sexual tool that's the same on both men and women. The idea of pressing those tools together, reports B. Taylor in the turn-of-the-century book *Northern Travel,* is downright indecent. Among certain Finnish people of that time, bathing nude together was perfectly acceptable, but kissing was not. When Taylor told one Finnish woman that it was common in his country for a husband to kiss his wife, she angrily replied, "If my husband were to attempt such a thing, faith, I would warm his ears in such a way that he would feel it for a whole week."

In 1951, anthropologists Clelland Ford and Frank Beach reported that the Thonga, the Lepcha, and the Balinese, among others, preferred to rub cheeks, because they regarded the mouth as a perilous device reserved for biting and chewing. And in *Strange Customs of Courtship and Marriage,* William J. Fielding noted that the Chinese considered

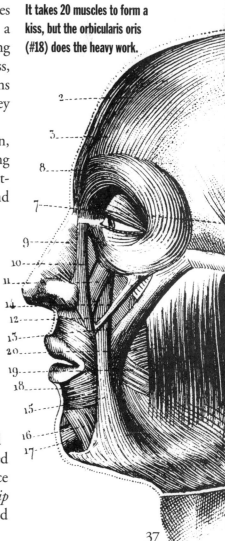

It takes 20 muscles to form a kiss, but the orbicularis oris (#18) does the heavy work.

37

the European kiss to be "suggestive of ravenous cannibals."

Cannibals! Our sixth-grade sex ed teacher hadn't mentioned cannibals. In fact, she hadn't mentioned a lot of important details — like how I was supposed to breathe. Three . . . two . . . one. Michael leaned his face in the direction of mine. I shut my eyes, stuck out my lips, and hoped I wouldn't die of suffocation.

A Lesson in Kissing Hygiene

Once upon an ancient time, storybooks told the tale of a young maiden who, from childhood, was fed small doses of lethal poisons to make her beautiful to look at but deadly to approach. She was sent by the enemies of Alexander the Great to the king's palace, in hopes that he would (literally) fall for her. But Aristotle, suspecting treachery, warned the king away and forced a sentenced criminal to kiss the girl instead. Sure enough, one kiss and the convict fell down dead, poisoned by the maiden's breath.

Rotten breath in most cases won't cause sudden death, but it will likely foster a social stigma. Capitalizing on that fear, early mouthwash ads played upon singles' insecurities. In 1880, Listerine presented an ad featuring the bad-breathed Herb — a bachelor, they told us, who's "an awfully nice fellow with some money . . . who plays a swell game of bridge," but who's "that way."

It is a problem that has clung to us like garlic to the tongue. Today as many as 25 million Americans suffer from chronic bad breath, says *Health* magazine, and many more have morning breath from time to time. Richard Price, a Massachusetts dentist who's spent a lot of time looking into a lot of mouths, tries to be understanding. "We all have dragon breath at some point," he says. "The only place where a person wakes up and kisses someone with sheer confidence is in the movies." (More on that later.)

While we sleep, our saliva production decreases. The lingering pools stagnate on the tongue, on the palate, and inside the cheek. While we dream of love, bacteria act out a less romantic task: they break the food particles and dead cell leftovers into sulfur compounds . . . like those of a skunk. Yes,

In many non-Western cultures, provocative lips are kept under wraps.

Kiss-and-Ride

Officials in Munich, Germany, have created special zones to prevent traffic tie-ups on busy highways. It seems that drivers kissing their spouses good-bye at the entrance to subway stations had created terrific traffic jams. Now signs marked "Kiss-and-Ride" make it so that "you don't have to chuck your husband or wife out of the car anymore," says a Munich official.

küssen

und fahren

a skunk. We wake in the morning to that unpleasant reality. Honey, there's something I've been meaning to tell you . . .

A Matter of Taste

"After your lips have been glued together for some time, open them slightly," advised author Hugh Morris in his 1936 book *The Art of Kissing*. "Then put the tip of your tongue out so that you can feel the smooth surface of your kissee's teeth. This will be a signal for her to respond in kind . . . she should project the tip of her tongue so that it meets with the tip of yours. Heaven will be in that union! Lava will run through your veins instead of blood. Your breath will come in short gasps. There will rise up in you an over-powering, overwhelming surge of emotion such as you have never experienced."

Not surprisingly, Mr. Morris considered the French kiss the most erotic form of osculation. Since then, scientists have probed the subject even more deeply. Writing in the *British Journal of Dermatology*, Dr. Bubba Nicholson explained that when we kiss, we are tasting the semiochemicals on our partner's skin. Those semiochemicals allow us to exchange pheromones (the chemical substances produced by the body to attract the opposite sex) and subconsciously sample the kissee for compatibility.

But according to zoologist Desmond Morris, the French kiss is a more primal and primitive sort of exchange, one that simulates the ancient practice of mothers when weaning their infants. Before food processors, the theory goes, women mashed food with their own teeth and pushed it directly with their tongues into their babies' mouths. As adults, we

From fresh katydid to French kiss — is our eroticism a Relic Gesture?

still take satisfaction from tongue kisses, because they evoke the sensual well-being of childhood nurturing. "This almost bird-like system of parental care seems strange and alien to us today," writes Morris, "but our species probably practiced it for a million years or more, and adult erotic kissing today is almost certainly a Relic Gesture."

Such an explanation would have done nothing, I'm certain, to put me at ease back in sixth grade when I experienced my first French kiss. I had just managed to turn my head enough from Michael's cheek to catch some air through one nostril, when I felt a wriggling on Michael's side of our walled lips. Embarrassed, I kept my mouth clamped shut. Later, I inquired discreetly among my girlfriends to find out what Michael had been doing. French kissing, they warned, was dangerous. They told me the story of the Italian vacationer who'd bitten off part of his wife's tongue during a passionate kiss in the back seat of a taxi in Patras, Greece. That's when I decided I'd had enough. I'd rather kiss a frog, I told Michael, than lick his tongue, or get mine bitten off. It was over between us.

The Toxicology of Love

It's been said that you have to kiss an awful lot of frogs before you find a prince. And that may be true. It's also been said, by F. Scott Fitzgerald, that "the kiss originated when the first male reptile licked the first female reptile, implying in a subtle, complimentary way that she was as succulent as the small reptile he had for dinner the night before." In either case, the idea is not appealing to a preadolescent. And maybe that's why the Frog Prince Tale, which took root in 13th-century Scotland, still remains popular today. The tale passed through many cultures and many variations before it was set down by the Brothers Grimm in Germany in 1812. The version most Americans know goes like this:

A princess drops her golden ball into a deep well and cries at having lost it. A frog appears from the water and says he will retrieve the ball if she promises to bring him to her castle, share her dinner, and allow him in her bed that night. The princess agrees, gets her ball back, and promptly forgets her promise. That night the frog appears, and although the princess wants nothing to do with him, the king insists that she keep her word. She eats with the frog. He follows her to her room. She kisses him (ugh!). He becomes a handsome prince (wow!). They marry and live (how else?) happily ever after.

Scientists such as David Siegel and Susan McDaniel at the University of Rochester, New York, have studied the biological and psychosocial implications of the Frog Prince Tale. They tell us the story has some connection to reality. Certain frogs, like the *Bufo marinus,* secrete a poisonous substance called bufotoxin or bufotenin on their skin to ward off predators. That substance, if licked by a human, causes visual and auditory hallucinations like those produced by LSD. Kissing a frog and seeing a prince, therefore, makes toxicological sense. But the tale also offers a healthy dose of sex education — a reassuring account about sexual awakening. As Siegel and McDaniel write, "The story assured children that sexuality that may seem disgusting (or frog-like) at one age will, at another, turn into something very beautiful, provided it happens at the right time and in the right way."

The right time never came for Michael and me. The following year, he left for Germany. The Germans, I've heard, have a saying that goes, "A kiss may indeed be washed away, but the fire in the heart cannot be quenched." I never heard whether Michael turned out to be a prince, but at the very least I can say that he, and his kisses, seem less froglike to me now. ♥

Don't Look Now!

"Kissing is a means of getting two people so close together," Rene Yasenek once said, "that they can't see anything wrong with each other." In fact, only 8 percent of 1,012 adults surveyed by Gallup said that they keep their eyes open when they kiss.

The classic Frog Prince Tale: The princess said she'd rather croak.

A Glossary of Kisses

By definition, a kiss takes two, so you'll want to find a friend before you read on . . .

Gerⁿ **dictionaries** list more than 30 types of kisses, including a word, *nachkussen,* for "the making up for kisses that have been omitted." Just imagine the types of kissing we've overlooked. Here are 20 variations you'll want to explore.

1. The Vacuum Kiss

Recommended in the 1936 manual *The Art of Kissing,* the Vacuum Kiss is performed by "sucking inward as though you were trying to draw out the innards of an orange." The powerful suction on the lips requires that the kiss must be brief. Be advised that when the lips have wearied, they should not be torn suddenly apart, or a loud smack will startle others nearby. Instead, gently loosen a corner of the mouth to release a faint hissing. If the kiss has been performed correctly, the manual notes, "a delicious sense of torpor will creep over your entire body, giving a lassitude that is almost beatific."

2. The Butterfly Flutter

Place your eye within a breath of your partner's cheek. Open and close your eyelids against her skin. If this is done correctly, the flutter sensation on her cheek should match the one in her heart.

3. The Earlobe Lap

You will do well to experiment with little sips of the lobe, but great control is recommended to avoid loud slurping — the erogenous ear is also

The secret to the Vacuum Kiss is suction.

42

an especially sensitized noise detector. (Take care not to swallow any earrings.)

4. The Talking Kiss

Sweet nothings whispered into the mouth are sweeter than those whispered into the ear, because the mouth is the preferred organ for tasting. If caught in the act, simply say, as Chico Marx did, "I wasn't kissing her. I was whispering into her mouth."

5. The Spying Kiss

To determine whether your mate has drunk an overabundance of wine.

6. The Hand Kiss

Historically, the Hand Kiss, with its required bow of subordination, showed deference to a lady. If a male was too superior to lower himself, he simply raised the woman's hand to his mouth. Since the Hand Kiss has now fallen out of fashion, it makes an unexpectedly romantic impression. To perform it cor-

For romance, the Hand Kiss is never out of fashion.

43

The Bumper Kiss might give your lover the jump-start he needs.

The Surprise Kiss could be your trump card.

rectly, lower your eyes and cup your shoulders over the lady's fingers, prolonging the moment when your lips rest on her hand. You will know the kiss has made its mark if the receiver avoids washing for several days to make sure the warm sensation stays sealed where your lips have placed it.

7. The Bumper Kiss

Effective when following your lover in a separate car. Wait till he stops his vehicle at a traffic light, then gently ease your car up to his and nudge his bumper. The jolt will jump-start his heart and suggest more intimate nuzzlings to come. (Warning: Do not use the Bumper Kiss on the vehicle of an unknown driver.)

8. The Surprise Kiss

This kiss takes place inadvertently during a parlor game called "Suck and Blow." To begin, gather men and women in a circle and try passing a playing card from mouth to mouth by first inhaling to receive the card and then exhaling to pass the card to the next person. If the pass is successful, you will be left feeling pleasantly lightheaded. If the pass is unsuccessful, the card will slip, leaving your lips pressed to those of your unsuspecting neighbor. (To cheat at this game, simply position yourself beside someone you would like to kiss and pretend you're having trouble mastering the technique.)

9. The Blown Kiss

In the book *Is Sex Necessary?* James Thurber and E. B. White contend that many men "would be perfectly willing to express their eroticism if it could be done at a reasonable distance — say fifty paces." For such frigid types, kissing, of course, presents a problem. They will find the Blown Kiss to be the most satisfactory.

10. The Mistletoe Kiss

Useful for those too shy to make the leap toward a potential lover's lips without a visible excuse.

11. The Forehead Kiss

Zoologist Desmond Morris claims that the Forehead Kiss is seen as mock-parental since a mother or father will often comfort a child with a kiss to the crown of his head.

Blushing Red Corn

In the old days, when country folks gathered to clean corn at a husking bee, the suitor who found a red ear of corn could claim the prize of a kiss from his favorite girl. It's said that sometimes the older farmers planted a few red ears in the pile to keep the youngsters interested.

Some Like It Scratchy

Everyone has his or her own favorite kiss. Germans, according to Dr. Christopher Nyrop's 1901 book *The Kiss and Its History*, like their kisses served with a side order of beard. "A kiss without a beard is like an egg without salt," they say. And "kissing a fellow without a quid of tobacco is like kissing a clay wall." Some slop, they seem to think, is appealing — but only to a point. A man who is "too wet about the mouth" is a man who is "nice to kiss [only] when one is thirsty."

12. The Eskimo Kiss

Contrary to popular belief, the Eskimo Kiss is not done merely to keep the lips from freezing together. In fact, some tribes in hot African countries rub or press noses in greeting and use a word for "kiss" that means "smell." In Malaysia, Charles Darwin reported the following: "The women squatted with their faces upturned; my attendants stood leaning over them, laid the bridge of their noses at right angles over theirs, and commenced rubbing. It lasted somewhat longer than a hearty handshake with us. During this process they uttered a grunt of satisfaction."

13. The Hickey Kiss

It may take some practice to create a personalized hickey in the shape of, say, your favorite sailing ship. No need to get fancy. The main objective is simply to avoid drawing blood while leaving a mark that will prove to your sweetheart (and all her girlfriends) that last night's interlude was not a dream.

14. The Electric Kiss

Choose a partner. Turn the lights down low. Shuffle wildly across the carpet until you've neared your partner in a sufficiently charged state. Lean slowly toward him, so that your lips are the first body parts to touch. Sparks will fly in the darkness. Avoid the natural inclination to pull away. After becoming accustomed to the shock, you may be inclined to increase the voltage with a battery-powered device or an electric socket. Resist the temptation.

15. The French Kiss

Some call this "The Soul Kiss," because the life and soul are thought to pass through the mouth's breath in the exchange across tongues. Surprisingly, the French call this "The English Kiss."

16. The Aunt Sally Special

A hearty smack to the cheek, done with puckered, slobbery, lipsticked lips. The female kisser should employ the Aunt Sally Special when a sobering note is needed during an escalating affair. If done right, this smooch will cause your partner to stop and wipe the spit off his cheek, which, in turn, will allow you time to fix your hair and adjust your skirt. After a calming rest period, relations may resume.

17. The Foot Kiss

People with ticklish feet will find the Foot Kiss quite funny, but just relax and enjoy it. Afterward, an extra touch of romance can be added by sending a little note signed "QBSP" (*Quien besa su pie*— "Who kisses your foot"), which once was the fashionable line with which to close correspondence in Spain.

18. The Nip Kiss

"Naturally, in the nip kiss the kisser is not supposed to open his mouth like the maw of a lion and then sink his fangs into the delicate flesh of the kissee," we are told in *The Art of Kissing*. "The procedure is the same as the ordinary kiss except that, instead of closing your lips with the kiss, you leave them slightly open, as though you were going to nibble on a delicious tidbit."

19. The Marathon Make-Out Kiss

In the words of Elizabeth Barrett Browning, it is "as long and silent as the ecstatic night."

20. The Last Kiss

In ancient Rome, custom had it that the Last Kiss would capture the soul of a dying man and keep it alive on the lips of his lover. ♥

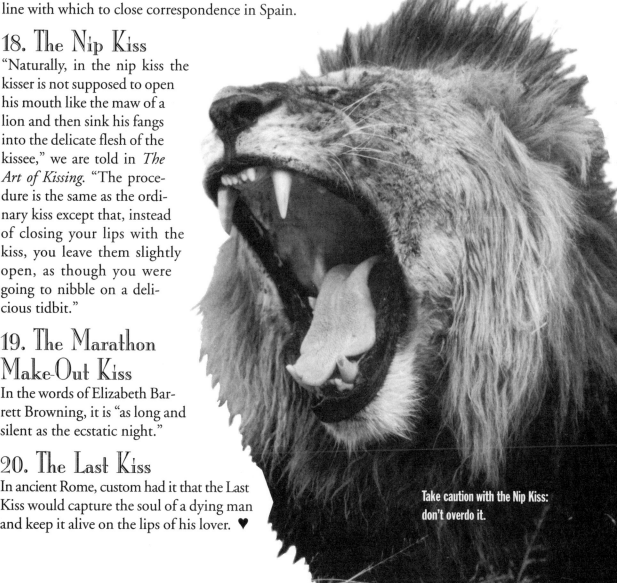

Take caution with the Nip Kiss: don't overdo it.

Kisses of the Silver Screen

In Hollywood's golden years, movie kisses were stilted, exaggerated, totally unrealistic. Frankly, my dear, we loved every one of them.

In the darkness, it's just you and Clark Gable (and the smell of popcorn and the sound of others shifting in their seats), and he tips your head back and tells you, "There's a soldier of the South who wants to love you, Scarlett (he calls you Scarlett, and you pretend), who wants to feel your arms around him, who wants to carry the memory of your kisses into battle with him. Never mind about loving me. Scarlett, kiss me. Kiss me." And you do (through the lips of Vivien Leigh), and you remember that kiss for always as an intimate moment you alone shared with Rhett in the dark.

But if the truth be known, that was not your kiss, but rather the most memorable movie kiss of all those polled by Gallup in 1992. And frankly, my dear, you were only one in a long line of ladies whom Clark Gable kissed on-screen. There were Greta Garbo and Ava Gardner, Doris Day and Fay Wray, Jean Harlow, Joan Crawford, Lana Turner, Deborah Kerr, Jane Russell, and, well, let's just say there were lots.

That most private of moments, when the camera moved in close, was only an illusion of intimacy. What made it work so well (besides the chemistry of the stars) was that you wanted it to work, wanted to believe in the passion of that kiss. Wanted to get carried away and forget

When Rhett kissed Scarlett, more sparks flew than in the burning of Atlanta.

The 1896 film *The Kiss* was a landmark in silent passion.

the crowd of people in the theater, forget the crowd of people it took to make the film in the first place — the director yelling "Cut," the cameramen making jokes, the makeup artist dabbing lipstick off Vivien's tooth. You wanted to be swept up in Rhett's strong arms and carried in your rustling gown up that wide staircase to the bedroom. And that's exactly what the guys who wrote the Motion Picture Production Code and those at the Legion of Decency office were afraid of. America's moral fabric, in their opinion, had been torn to shreds by the loose standards of movies in the 1920s — and even earlier.

The Hazardous History of Movie Kisses

It had started as early as 1896, when a silent film called *The Kiss* had May Irwin and John C. Rice lock lips in history's first motion picture kiss. In retrospect, it wouldn't look like much. One film critic would later write, "Their kiss suggested not so much the heat of passion as a mishap involving dry ice or Krazy Glue." But at the time, the reel passed for erotica and caused outrage among many upright citizens. "The spectacle of their prolonged pasturing on each other's lips was hard to bear," wrote Chicago publisher Herbert S. Stone. "Such things call for police interference."

By the beginning of the Roaring Twenties, legislators across the country were proposing bills that would censor movies and stem the flood of corruption. But by this time, moviemaking had become a big business that couldn't afford federal interference. To forestall government censorship by proving that they could police their own industry, the producers joined in 1922 with Postmaster General Will Hays (a strict Presbyterian with ties to the White House) and formed the Motion Picture Producers and Distributors of America. The organization members created their own set of moral guidelines for motion pictures and called it the Production Code. Only those movies that passed the association's criteria, formally implemented in 1934, went forth to the viewing public with the Production Code Seal of Approval. Those that didn't pass were banned, and if the producer attempted to distribute the film without the seal, he would be fined. What's more, a Roman Catholic Church group called the Legion of Decency imposed its own three-letter rating on films for Catholics' well-being: *A* for "morally unobjectionable," *B* for "morally objectionable," and *C* for "positively bad" or "condemned."

Seduction in the Dark

Believing that uncensored movies could taint American values, Production Code administrator Joseph Breen fought hard against scenes that included vulgarity, profanity, religious ridicule, criminal conduct, and, of course, sex. The code he enforced so rigorously proclaimed that "the sanctity of the institution of marriage and the home shall be upheld. Pictures shall not infer that low forms of sexual relationship are the accepted or common thing."

The code forced screenwriters to be clever where they weren't clean and to resort to fireworks bursting in the night sky, waves crashing on the beach, or brief kisses fading to black. But the censors soon caught on. ". . . we suggest that you fade out immediately [when] he starts to carry her up the stairs," Breen ruled on *Gone With the Wind*, "rather than prolong the 'fade.'" In the darkness, minds might wander . . .

Clearly, this was cause for concern. When it came to "Scenes of Passion," the following rules applied: "a.) They should not be introduced when not essential to the plot. b.) Excessive and lustful kissing, lustful embraces,

Sealed with a Kiss

The custom of signing a letter with an X to signify a kiss began in the early Christian era at a time when it was common for someone who couldn't write to sign his name with a cross. To prove his sincerity, the signer often kissed the mark as he would kiss the Bible to seal an oath. That habit of kissing the X has been handed down to us, and the X alone now symbolizes the kiss.

In the darkness, minds might wander . . . *From Here to Eternity*.

suggestive postures and gestures, are not to be shown. c.) In general passion should so be treated that these scenes do not stimulate the lower and baser element."

Holding Back the Damn

Gone With the Wind as it was first scripted stirred too many of those base emotions. Intent on softening the steamy relationship between Rhett and Scarlett, Breen fired off a memo to the producer, advising that Rhett be less rough with Scarlett. Rhett, Breen suggested, should "take [Scarlett] in his arms, kiss her, and then gently start with her toward the bedroom. It is our thought that you should not go so far as to throw her on the bed." Nor should he say to Scarlett, "I want you," but rather, "I think more of you." In the final scene, Breen said, the profanity would have to go. The closing dialogue needed a moral polish. He suggested this exchange:

Scarlett: "Oh, my darling, if you go, what shall I do?"

Rhett: "My dear, I don't care."

Luckily for us, the director, frankly, didn't give a damn for Breen's ruling. After a stormy exchange and some compromises, Breen backed down on that final word. He amended the code to allow for "damn" in cases where it had been picked up from a literary work. It was the beginning of the end for Breen. By 1968, the code would give way to the *G* through *X* ratings of the Motion Picture Association of America. But *Gone With the Wind* would hang on as having the number one best kiss in the minds of American viewers.

Coming in at number two was the beach scene between Deborah Kerr and Burt Lancaster in *From Here to Eternity*. Viewed today, it doesn't look like much — their lips barely meet — but what is so suggestive (or seemed so at the time) is that they are in swimsuits and a wave washes over them. After the wave, they jump up, run to higher ground, fling themselves on beach towels, and try to talk of love. The words come off as forced flirtation.

"I never thought it could be like this," says Karen. "Nobody ever kissed me the way you do."

"Nobody?" Warden asks.

"No, nobody."

"Not even one, out of all the men you've been kissed by?"

"Now, that'd take some figuring," says Karen. "How many do you think there have been?"

"I wouldn't know," says Warden. "Can't you give me a rough estimate?"

"Not without an adding machine. Do you have your adding machine with you?"

No, of course not. They're on a beach. No one brings an adding machine to the beach. Where would you plug it in? In the old movies,

The Dark Side of Mistletoe

Everyone knows the fun custom of kissing the man or woman who stands beneath the mistletoe. But not everyone knows the darker traits of the plant itself. Mistletoe is a clinging parasite, which roots its way into deciduous and evergreen trees, often killing its host. Certain mistletoe berries can poison a person or animal who ingests them, and the leaves can cause stillbirths among cattle that eat them. Better to taste only a lover's lips.

romance could be awkward and silly. A kiss could cover corny lines.

"Here's looking at you, kid," Humphrey Bogart says to Ingrid Bergman in *Casablanca*. That line used by a guy in a New York bar today would sound slightly patronizing or macho. But in that same Gallup poll, we ranked the *Casablanca* kiss that followed as the third most memorable in movie history. We sensed that the tough guy had turned soggy as cereal in milk. And we felt it, too.

Lips Larger Than Life

There in the flickering dark, we could find role models to show us how to kiss and carry on. Everyone on the silver screen looked, literally, bigger than life. And we had a chance to see up close what worked for men and for women. What looked good for actresses were rosebud-shaped or Cupid's bow–type lips. Marilyn Monroe and Greta Garbo embodied the ideal: when they pouted their fat red lips, we saw youth and beauty. We trusted that how they kissed was how we should, too.

If Hollywood kisses were stilted in the first half of the 1900s, maybe it's because *we* were. "The old-fashioned Hollywood movie kiss," said one radio commentator, "required the two stars to mash their faces together as though they had a walnut pinned in there and were trying to crack it." But were we any better? Men on the screen and off were supposed to be remote, so tough guys like Humphrey Bogart suggested glamour behind a smoke screen of coolness. "Bogart taught generations how to hold a cigarette," says film critic Lance Morrow, "how to inhale, how to squint through the smoke. But as a kisser Bogart was an awful example. His mouth addressed a woman's lips with the quivering nibble of a horse closing in on an apple." Put Bogart in the no-smoking section of Rick's Café Americaine today, and he wouldn't seem so sexy. Without the dramatic backlighting and the sensual mood music, Hollywood romance seems only ridiculous. "Rudolph Valentino was among those who favored a hyperbolic style," notes Morrow. "Arching the woman into a circumflex, he'd do a semaphore with his eyebrows. He had the technique of a gifted and tormented periodontist." All that mattered was that they were doing it — kissing before our eyes.

Cornball sentiment could steal the show. Maybe because we were more innocent in 1942, when a classic

Driving Under the Influence (of Love)

The Italians now have a legal ban on drivers kissing or embracing while at the wheel. The part about ear nibbling, we're told, is enforced with particular strictness.

like *Ball of Fire* could have a character named Sugarpuss gush: "He looks like a giraffe and I love him. I love him because he's the kind of guy who gets drunk on a glass of buttermilk, and I love the way he blushes right up over his ears. I love him because he doesn't know how to kiss — the jerk!"

In the old days, a movie could say it all with a kiss and a fade to black. But over time, we wanted to see more. And we got it. And we got it. And we got it. Kisses became only a blinking yellow light on the speedway toward sex. And sex on-screen became such

A kiss is just a kiss . . . ?

a given — so much, so fast — that romance lost its mystery. The only thing left out was our imagination.

In the summer of 1985, an outside censor was no longer needed to rule on steamy kisses — those inside Hollywood had found their own reason to protest against them. A passionate kiss between Rock Hudson and Linda Evans on the television show *Dynasty* led to considerable controversy when Hudson later disclosed that he had AIDS. Fear spread that others might, too. That fall, the Screen Actors Guild notified seven thousand producers and agents that from then on actors should be alerted ahead of time about any open-mouthed kissing scenes they were required to do. Heavy kissing scenes now came under the "danger" clause.

Eventually, actors and actresses did everything in bed together *but* kiss. To kiss, says Julia Roberts's character in *Pretty Woman,* is out of the question during sex, because it would mean that she and Richard Gere's character had gone too far. Later in the movie, when they do kiss, we know it isn't just about sex, it's about falling in love. We see that a kiss still says it all. And we know that the fundamental things still apply, as time goes by . . . ♥

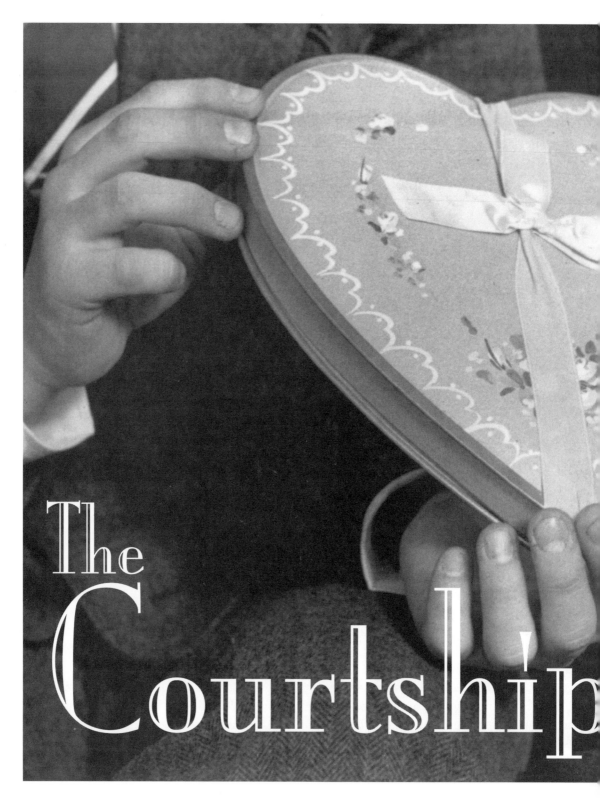

The
Courtship

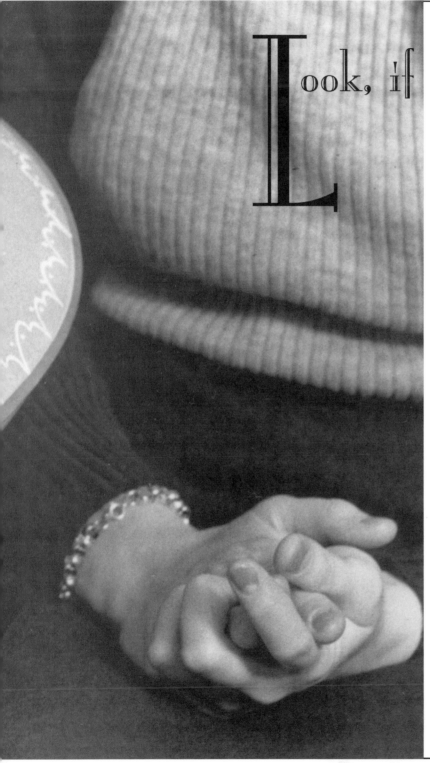

Look, if animals

as low-down as salamanders can do it, humans can, too. In recent years, we at *The Old Farmer's Almanac* have been saddened to note a slight decline in the gentlemanly art of courtship. In an effort to resurrect that fine and ancient practice, we include here some inspiration: the story of three early 19th-century bachelors in love with a single girl named Lydia; a springtime ode to courtship in the animal kingdom; a lesson in love-letter writing from King Henry VIII and other notables; and the history of courtship, from bundling to the back seat. If you don't learn anything else, you should at least remember what the animals know about courtship: be flashy, be affectionate, but don't be off-key.

Why Salamanders Cross the Road

And other romantic riddles of spring.

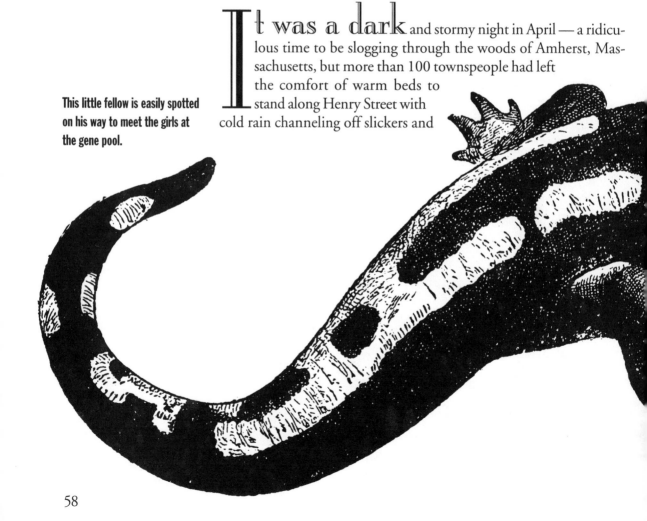

This little fellow is easily spotted on his way to meet the girls at the gene pool.

It was a dark and stormy night in April — a ridiculous time to be slogging through the woods of Amherst, Massachusetts, but more than 100 townspeople had left the comfort of warm beds to stand along Henry Street with cold rain channeling off slickers and red flashlights pointed at the ground. What they hoped to see were spotted salamanders — big ones, about eight inches long — emerging from the earth and making their way north to mate in a vernal pool about half a mile away. Nothing was guaranteed for these rain-drenched onlookers. Chances were good that they would miss the moment, that they would go home cold and exhausted for work or school the next day having seen only mud and wet leaves and half the neighborhood in soggy shoes. Still, they parked their cars along Henry Street and waited.

They knew that this oddity of nature takes place only once a year, for only a few hours, when the sound and smell of the first spring rain shakes the creatures from their yearlong slumber and fills them with unstoppable lust. In recent years, as Henry Street had gotten busier, more salamanders had gotten squashed in their run to reproduce. The salamanders' predicament had become flat-out obvious, and the crowds at first had come for the novelty of it. They'd carried the wriggling salamanders across the road or slowed the passing cars so that the creatures didn't get crushed. But then, in 1988, Robert Winston (a.k.a. "Commander Salamander") had helped orga-nize a

☞ **From The** ☜
Old Farmer's Almanac

Converse always with your female friends as if a gentleman were of the party, and with young men as if your female companions were present.

— 1858

59

brigade to ensure safe sex for salamanders. Together with other townspeople, he put up "Salamander Crossing" signs, constructed a funneling fence, and built a special "love tunnel" so that the salamanders could crawl under the road to safety without human help. It worked.

The townspeople could have stayed home that year, and the following years for that matter, but they preferred to get wet watching the salamanders. It had become a ritual of sorts, a passage into spring. Seeing the salamanders court may have stirred a longing for similar activity among the onlookers. But all they would say was "Wow, would you look at that."

Human help, in the form of special signs on Henry Street, ensured safe sex for Amherst salamanders.

With a shake of dirt, the creatures, one by one, poked their bodies out from under the mud and leaves. On crooked legs, each propelled himself down the hill — a bowlegged cowboy on a mission to mate. Strapped on like pistols, he carried two Q-Tip–like semen cones. Onward he charged, over roots and leaves and clumps of dirt, as unwavering as the raging runoff of spring. All around him, others followed suit, ready for a fling. Through the finely engineered tunnel they went, cheered on by spectators, then on across a neighboring yard, over the railroad tracks, and down the spongy bank. With a small splash, they entered the murky waters.

The Gene Pool of Love

In the pond, which would vanish by summer, no fishy predators lived. And to that pond, within a day's time, would come a cluster of females to join the boys for a round of reproduction. While they waited, the eager males deposited a practice round of semen cones. Later, when the females arrived, the males would dance in courtship, swimming up and down and wriggling wildly. The spots on their backs would flash like the white semen clumps they placed on the pond bottom, and eventually the females would join their eggs to the sperm clusters. The male and female salamanders would then go off in separate directions, leaving the little salamanders to take form on their own.

Having done their business, the males would march on home — up the bank, over the tracks, across the yard, through the tunnel, up the hill, and back underground again — ending the most taxing week of their lives. They'd let the whole cumbersome business slip from their reptilian minds . . . until it rained again in spring.

As for the onlookers, they'd go home pleased. Most would consider it a very messy but fairly miraculous night. "You know," one man later concluded, "it makes you think: if it can happen to them, it could happen to us." A temperature change, a shift of light, warm rain, and — bam! — it's time to go out courting.

Birds get pretty lightheaded and lusty in spring, but you would too if you had a paper-thin skull.

A Peculiar Disease

We call it spring fever because something akin to a disease rages through us and racks us with what *Merriam Webster's Collegiate Dictionary* calls "a lazy or restless feeling often associated with the onset of spring." Increasing sunlight is largely to blame for those sudden surges of energy, that angst, that unfounded gaiety, that unexplained leaping and singing behavior. We say a person acting that way is "mad as a March hare," because spring makes female brown hares chase males around and cuff their faces and ears.

Spring fever peaks more quickly in birds because they have paper-thin skulls, and the sun shines right

A springtime surge of energy, angst, or gaiety could make you as mad as a March hare.

through. A red-winged blackbird exposed to more hours of daylight will automatically start building a nest. That's all you need — a little extra light — and life changes in a fundamental way. A greenfinch exposed to a fake 7-hour "day" followed by 17 hours of "night" will sprout extra tissue on his testes. (Don't try this at home.) Add another 7 hours and — presto! — that lonely little bird has become a regular sperm factory.

It happens in female greenfinches, too. If you increase the greenfinch's photoperiods, her ovaries swell in anticipation of sex. And instead of flying off at the sight of a male, she'll head straight toward

him in hot pursuit. Sure enough, sunlight has shifted her hormonal tide right on cue with his — leaving them both as close as can be to the two proverbial love-birds in a tree.

In humans and other mammals, the process happens through the optic nerve. Light passes through it to the pineal gland (what science writer Mark Walters calls "the clock keeper for seasonal breeding") at the center of the brain. Without the pineal gland, animals' mating systems would get thrown off kilter — sheep would breed out of season, and Syrian hamsters would take over the earth. But luckily, we have seasonal controls that work like this: In spring, lengthening days cue the pineal gland to stop making the melatonin block and instead send luteinizing hormones to the ovaries and testes. The testes, in turn, fire off testosterone and other hormones, which make males aggressive, stimulate stags' antlers to grow, inspire men to court women, and that sort of thing.

As it goes in the animal kingdom, so it goes among humans. Not surprisingly, more babies are conceived in spring than at any other time of year. In the midst of mud season, our deadened love sensors suddenly awake. They fire off red-alert signals when the opposite sex is spotted. You'd think that living in a world of controlled light and temperature would make us immune to seasonal shifts, but it doesn't. In spring, we need less energy for sheer survival; we can shed cumbersome clothes, pick up our heads from the pavement, look around, and see the sexiness of each other again. We find ourselves exchanging pleasantries out of unaccountable good cheer. (Nice day. Say, what are you doing for dinner? Shall we follow it with sex?) Everywhere you look, it's a coupling convention. The planet tilts, and we are tipped toward romance. We chase each other like rabbits, charge downhill like salamanders.

Courting Cues from the Animal Kingdom

Darwin pointed out that males can succeed in one of two ways: by winning a female or conquering the competition. But conquering the competition, in our view, is only the beginning of winning the female.

Come spring, testosterone levels rise and males fight to the finish for a female's affection.

The pit viper, for instance, fights at first to defeat a competing male, but then must spend hours seducing the female — stroking his chin against her scaly skin and flicking his tongue over her long, slinky body.

The point is that animals, like people, will go to great lengths to prove they are something special. Bullfrogs will serenade through the night; bank swallows will pass a white feather back and forth during flight despite the danger of attracting hawks with what might as well be a white "We're Open for Dinner" flag. The courtship dance is made even sweeter by the fact that those doing it are made vulnerable in the act. The male hummingbird hovers and swings like a pendulum before his sweetheart; rising in a swooping arch, he performs airborne figure eights, which inspire the female to join him in a swoop 100 feet high. Although we humans can't reach such heights in actual flight, we go there in our hearts.

After all, who wouldn't be inspired by the springtime behavior of the most romantic feathered species? Take the performance of the colorful long-tailed manakin. Perched on a limb above the rain forest floor, two male manakins perform a duet for the female. Singing "toe-le-doe," the males hop up and down, leapfrogging each other, fluttering their wings, and wildly whipping their tail feathers. The tempo rises to a frenzy, until the dominant male lets out a shrill note and circles the female. (This is a finale sure to impress everyone except the second-string male, who suddenly finds himself superfluous.) It is spring, when longings are stirred and each suitor learns how best to win over his mate.

Perhaps the most enthralling love song of all lies deep in the ocean. At the start of each breeding season, the humpback whale bellows the same serenade that he and the other whales ended with the year before. Then, over the

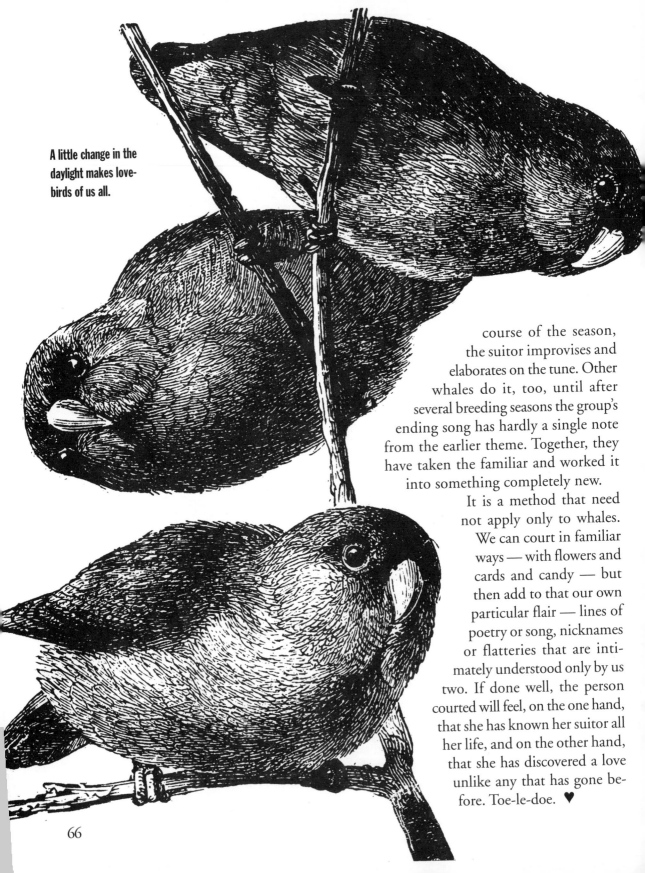

A little change in the daylight makes love-birds of us all.

course of the season, the suitor improvises and elaborates on the tune. Other whales do it, too, until after several breeding seasons the group's ending song has hardly a single note from the earlier theme. Together, they have taken the familiar and worked it into something completely new.

It is a method that need not apply only to whales. We can court in familiar ways — with flowers and cards and candy — but then add to that our own particular flair — lines of poetry or song, nicknames or flatteries that are intimately understood only by us two. If done well, the person courted will feel, on the one hand, that she has known her suitor all her life, and on the other hand, that she has discovered a love unlike any that has gone before. Toe-le-doe. ♥

A Time of Wanton Dalliance

It is no surprise that modern dictionaries define spring as the season of procreation and renewal, but it is interesting to note that people as long ago as 1398 remarked on spring's rousing effect. Printed uses of "springtime" back then said the season was the time when the world "leaps to its feet and new life springs from the ground." Since prehistoric times, cultures all over the world have staged fertility rites to welcome spring: The Babylonians acted out myths of Creation; the ancient Greeks honored the god of love during the Festival of Flowers; the Romans celebrated flora and sexuality; the Christians had Lent, which stemmed from old pagan traditions of self-denial thought to help spring's resurgence; May Day most likely evolved from the fertility festivals of India and Egypt and got translated into England's celebration of young adults. The English youths brought branches and flowers from the woods after engaging in wanton dalliances.

How to Write a Love Letter

A lesson from King Henry VIII and friends.

Why, you say, should anyone bother writing a love letter when the telephone will do just as well? First, we say, because no one can carry a call in her pocket, pulling it out to savor by day and memorize by night. Second, it will mean more to her that you took the time to find paper and pen and spill your heart out in ink. Third, you'll most likely get a letter in return, and then you, too, can have the thrill of finding not another bill in your box, but a red-hot letter. It may well be enough to put you in that state of love-letter ecstasy described by Edith Wharton: "The first glance to see how many pages there are, the second to see how it ends, the breathless first reading, the slow lingering over each phrase and each word, the taking possession, the absorbing of them, one by one, and finally the choosing of the one that will be carried in one's thoughts all day, making an exquisite accompaniment to the dull prose of life."

What you want to do when you write a love letter, according to the 1936 manual *How to Make Love,* is "imagine that your loved one is seated next to you on the sofa and that you are whispering things to her. Write them down on a paper (never typewrite them because type is too impersonal for as personal a missive as a love letter)." Whatever you do, the manual further notes, don't write the letter as though it were a guidebook, and don't mention the indigestion you suffered last

night. Try instead to link whatever is happening to you now to some memory of what the two of you have shared in the past or will share in the future. For example, if you are away on a business trip, you might write something like what follows, written from one fellow to his "Darling Anne": "I go about my business here, I talk about 'carpet tacks and sealing wax' but, in my mind, there is only the picture of a little girl with dark brown hair and big black eyes and with two quivering lips that almost make me want to drop everything and rush back home to her. But, no, I force myself to remain and try to sell 'carpet tacks and sealing wax' so that we can save enough toward that little cottage in Elmwood we've talked so much about."

For those who still find themselves at a loss for words, remember that three little ones will always do in a pinch. (No, not "Please send cookies," but "I love you.") The Prince de Joinville, after seeing Rachel Félix act in 1840, managed splendidly with just four little words sent on the back of his card: "Where? — When? — How much?" To which Rachel replied with four of her own: "Your place — Tonight — Free."

Sometimes that's all that need be said. And if even that fails, you can always resort to plagiarism. Take care, though, to choose a letter that isn't well-known. Antonia Fraser, who compiled *Love Letters, An Anthology* (where the following letters and more can be found), tells us that her father, while courting her mother, was known to (incorrectly) recite from Alfred Lord Tennyson's poem "The Princess": "Now falls the crimson petal, now the white." After which he would say solemnly: "I wrote that." According to Fraser, "He was felt to have gone rather far in his assumption of her [mother's] ignorance of English literature." But be that as it may, his plagiarizing must have worked, because she married him.

We wish you as well with your own love letters and leave you now to the masters.

A well-composed love letter will be saved (and savored) forever.

Henry didn't start out as a pain in the neck.

1 "My mistress and friend" demonstrates a relationship that has depth in both the sexual and platonic realms; also, by avoiding the use of her name, this salutation allows the adulterous writer to escape rebuke should the letter be discovered.

2 "I and my heart put ourselves in your hands" is the perfect way to act humble and also subtly suggest something a little sexual.

3 Absence is always a good word to use, since she will inevitably be wondering whether the heart has grown fonder or — as is so often the case — has slipped into that "out of sight, out of mind" state.

4 Mentioning the stars is a tried-and-true romantic trick. This reference is particularly clever because it is not only philosophical but also astronomically correct. It is sure to win points with the lady (even if she doesn't quite understand what you're getting at).

5 Never assume that your loved one feels as you do.

Letter One

You will notice in the following 1528 missive from King Henry VIII to Anne Boleyn that his letter is one long, long sentence. While this is effective to give the sensation of the mounting pressure of love, we recommend that you avoid the technique if you are courting an English teacher or editor.

My mistress and friend, [1]

I and my heart put ourselves in your hands, [2] *begging you to recommend us to your good grace and not to let absence lessen your affection, for it were great pity to increase their pain, seeing that absence* [3] *does that sufficiently and more than I could ever have thought possible; reminding us of a point of astronomy, which is that the longer the days are the farther off is the sun and yet the hotter;* [4] *so is it with our love, for although by absence we are parted it nevertheless keeps its fervency, at least in my case and hoping the like of yours;* [5] *assuring you that for myself the pang of absence is already too great, and when*

I think of the increase of what I must needs suffer it would be well nigh intolerable but for my firm hope of your unchangeable affection; [6] *and sometimes to put you in mind of this, and seeing that in person I cannot be with you, I send you now something most nearly pertaining thereto that is at present possible to send, that is to say, my picture set in a bracelet* [7] *with the whole device which you already know; wishing myself in their place when it shall please you. This by the hand of*

Your loyal servant and friend,

H Rex [8]

[6] In other words, he would die without her. Martyrdom, as Romeo and Juliet proved, adds a great touch of sentiment. (We'd recommend, however, that you not carry through with it.)

[7] Sending little presents is always a good bet, especially expensive ones if you can afford them. The picture is a nice touch, too. A lock of hair will do just as well if you're not so good to look at.

[8] "H Rex." Now isn't that sweet? A king called Rex. And what's more, a king who calls himself "your loyal servant and friend." Acting humble when you have a whole kingdom full of servants is sure to put you in good stead with the lady.

King Henry VIII's love letter, as you may have heard, effectively seduced Anne Boleyn. The good news is that after six years of obsession for her, he divorced Catherine of Aragon and made Anne his wife. The bad news is that when Anne couldn't bear him a son, he accused her of treason and adultery and had her tried and executed. In the meantime, he began a flirtation with another woman, whom he promptly married after Anne's death. The moral of the story? The guy was a jerk, but his love letters weren't bad.

⌐ From The ¬
Old Farmer's Almanac

Southern accents may be the sexiest, but Boston accents are the smartest. Those are two results of a survey conducted for Hyundai Motor America. In addition to being the sexiest, southern accents were also the most liked and most recognizable.

—1996

Letter Two

Here's one from Voltaire at The Hague in 1713 to Olympe Dunoyer. You'll notice the letter is made more romantic by the fact that it's written from a hotel where Voltaire had been unjustly imprisoned. If you can't manage to get yourself in an equally heart-wrenching predicament, you might at least make out that you've been imprisoned in some other way — in your parents' house, for instance, or in your office or your car (having run out of gas). In any case, tell your love you'll come to her rescue just as soon as you make your own escape. (Then call a tow truck.)

I am a prisoner here in the name of the King; they can take my life, but not the love that I feel for you.[9] *Yes, my adorable mistress, to-night I shall see you, and if I had to put my head on the block to do it.*[10] *For Heaven's sake, do not speak to me in such disastrous terms as you write; you must live and be cautious;*[11] *beware of madame your mother as of your worst enemy.*[12] *What do I say? Beware of everybody, trust no one;*[13] *keep yourself in readiness, as soon as the moon is visible; I shall leave the hotel incognito, take a carriage or a chaise, we shall drive like the wind*[14] *to Scheveningen; I shall take paper and ink with me; we shall write our letters. If you love me, reassure yourself, and call all your strength and presence of mind to your*

9 "They can take my life, but not the love that I feel for you." Perfect. Feel free to plagiarize that line yourself. It's that old Romeo-and-Juliet trick again. Lovers just can't get enough of that sort of thing.

10 See what we mean?

11 Of course, it's okay for you to sacrifice yourself, but when your loved one threatens to do something rash, you should jump immediately to her defense and tell her to be cautious.

12 The "mother-in-law as worst enemy" syndrome. A fairly predictable phrase. You'll want to avoid this tactic if your girlfriend actually likes her mom.

13 "Trust no one." Using a phrase like that creates an "us-against-them" drama, which binds you in bliss to your loved one forever (or at least until you find yourself wishing you had someone else to go bowling with).

14 "Drive like the wind" is a cliché, but lovers tend not to be overly critical of such things. Feel free to use a few yourself.

aid; do not let your mother notice anything, try to have your picture, and be assured that the menace of the greatest tortures will not prevent me to serve you. No, nothing has the power to part me from you; our love is based upon virtue, and will last as long as our lives. [15] *Adieu, there is nothing that I will not brave for your sake; you deserve more than that. Adieu,*[16] *my dear heart!*

   Arouet

Although the lovers managed to flee to Scheveningen, the authorities soon tracked them down and split them apart. Olympe's mother forced her to wed a well-to-do count, while Voltaire was shipped to Paris to toil in a lawyer's office. His letter-writing background, we imagine, added a romantic flair to what would otherwise have been very dull law briefs.

Letter Three

What follows is one of literally thousands of letters that Franz Kafka wrote to Felice Bauer after meeting her in 1912. Throughout the course of their correspondence, Franz proposed to her twice, and then twice broke it off. His indecision made her miserable and filled him with angst. But angst (as any good country-and-western writer knows) is the cornerstone of great love letters (and lyrics). If nothing else, unrequited love retains a dramatic edge that numerous humdrum marriages never do.

Fraulein Felice![17]

   . . . Write to me only once a week, so that your letter ar-

Kafka wished the situation could metamorphose.

18 Now here's a nice trick — a little reverse psychology. Say that you cannot bear to get more than one letter a week from your love, because her letters so exhaust you with emotion that you cannot even get out of bed. (This is especially appropriate coming from a man who will write a whole book as a bedridden cockroach.)

19 When even the clothes of your lover make you crazy, you know you've really lost it. Think twice before admitting this to her; she may start to feel as Miss Piggy does: "When you are in love with someone, you want to be near him all the time, except when you are out buying things and charging them to him."

20 While the act of "leaping on to a train with my eyes shut and opening them only when I am with you" may be a romantic notion that you'd like to incorporate into your own letter, we do not advise the actual practice of such an idea, for certainly doing so would leave you vulnerable to pickpockets, muggers, and the like, and, if nothing else, would result in a nasty bump on the head when you leap onto the train.

21 Here again is that notion of sacrificing it all for love. Sort of a good note to end on if you've just said you won't marry the girl, father her children, or do any of that important stuff that comes along with the romance package.

rives on Sunday — for I cannot endure your daily letters, I am incapable of enduring them.[18] *For instance, I answer one of your letters, then lie in bed in apparent calm, but my heart beats through my entire body and is conscious only of you. I belong to you; there is really no other way of expressing it, and that is not strong enough. But for this very reason I don't want to know what you are wearing; it confuses me so much that I cannot deal with life;* [19] *and that's why I don't want to know that you are fond of me. If I did, how could I, fool that I am, go on sitting in my office, or here at home, instead of leaping on to a train with my eyes shut and opening them only when I am with you?* [20] *Oh, there is a sad, sad reason for not doing so. To make it short: My health is only just good enough for myself alone, not good enough for marriage, let alone fatherhood. Yet when I read your letter, I feel I could overlook even what cannot possibly be overlooked. . . . If we value our lives, let us abandon it all.* [21]

Franz.

As good as his letters were, Franz could not follow through and "abandon it all." It wasn't until 1917, when he learned he had tuberculosis, that he finally found the resolve to end his affair with Felice.

Letter Four

OK, we'll make this one short and sweet. Johann Wolfgang von Goethe writes to Charlotte Buff in Frankfurt in 1774. He tells her she is everything. And since she truly *is* everything, there's not much else to write, now is there?

. . . and it seemed to me, that your spirit was about me, and about Karlinchen and Lenchen, everyone, and everything I had not seen, and had seen, and finally there was Lotte,[22] *and Lotte and Lotte,* [23] *and Lotte, and Lotte,*[24] *and without Lotte nothing but Want and Mourning and Death.*[25] *Adieu, Lotte, not a word more to-day, 26th August.*[26]

In conclusion, we can only say that, above all, you must be honest in your love letters. Even if at first it seems you have written something more harsh than romantic, your words in the end will ring true. Take, for one final instance, the letter of Bertrand Russell to Ottoline Morrell in March of 1911: "I did not know I loved you till I heard myself telling you so — for one instant I thought 'Good God, what have I said?' and then I knew it was the truth." What a wonderful way to convince your sweetheart that you really do love her. In fact, you might want to write that down yourself — and swear you just made it up. ♥

[22] Nicknames, by the way (such as "Lotte" for "Charlotte") make love letters special; their uniqueness provides extra reassurance that the letters haven't simply been recycled from a lover's last affair.

[23] Repetition is effective for showing her she is everything.

[24] Repetition is effective for showing her she is everything.

[25] "Want and Mourning and Death," the three biggies. If she can knock those three down, she must really be something special.

[26] "Not a word more to-day," followed by the date, locks your words in time and suggests that there will be more to come the next day and the next and the next and so on ever after.

Goethe missed her a Lotte.

From the Bedroom to the Buick & Back Again

Every time period has had its preferred location for

courtship — the bedroom, the parlor, the drive-in,

the den, the bedroom . . .

And now a days there are two ways,
Which of the two is right,
To lie between sheets sweet and clean,
Or sit up all the night?
— Henry Reed Stiles,
Bundling: Its Origin, Progress and Decline in America

One day, in the mid-1770s, a young man walked 10 miles on a Sabbath evening to his sweetheart's house. He arrived after dark at the door of the family's small Cape. The girl's parents welcomed in their daughter's suitor and led him through the cold, unlit front room to the bedroom. There in the feather bed their daughter sat, waiting. Beneath a goose-down quilt, she wore a modest, legged nightdress, fastened at the neck and waist with secure knots. Removing only his boots, the young man climbed into bed beside his sweetheart. The parents placed a bundling board between the two, confirmed their comfort, and retired to their own bed across the room. The two young people conversed quietly for a time, ran out of things to say, and promptly fell asleep.

By sunrise, the suitor had slipped from the girl's bed and hiked 10 miles home through the darkness. He worked hard that week, though not without distraction. His love for the girl had enveloped his heart like the folds of her feather bed. Granted, it was a cumbersome affair — so many clothes, so many reminders that the parents were nearby — but it beat shivering in the cold or wasting firewood and candles. It was a practical, Puritan affair, sanctioned by parental consent and backed by religious training. For the most part, it kept the young couple on their respective sides of the bed. In the early 17th century, courting undercover had been as common as eating at the table — it made sense. And it would have continued without question, except that matters of the human heart seldom avoid human gossip.

Sometime around 1756, bundling scholar Henry Reed Stiles tells us, city dwellers in places such as Salem, Newport, and New York had taken it upon themselves to forbid bundling among their sons

Though a board was laid between them, their love crossed the divide.

GIAM

77

Parlor courtship required the suitor to maneuver carefully through an obstacle course of etiquette.

and daughters. They lobbied for the sofa to become the preferable place to court. Rural folks disagreed and held to "old-fashioned" bundling practices. They said that fast-talking city folks engaged in far more shenanigans on sofas than country folks did in bed. A sofa, the rural population believed, was an uncouth Turkish import, suggestive of harems.

Two decades later, the two factions still tussled, like stubborn lovers who couldn't agree. A city clergyman who went to the country in 1776 to preach high-mindedly against the unchristian custom of bundling was told off by a crowd of wholesome rural women who took offense. The poor priest begged pardon, promised to change his sermon, and stole off. But he had succeeded in planting the seeds of suspicion, and by the turn of the century, bundling would be on its way out.

Out of the Bedroom, into the Parlor

Parlor courtship would take its place, and the shift from the bed to the sofa would make courtship a more formal and chilly affair. No longer could a young man arrive unannounced at the end of the day and crawl into bed with his sweetheart. Instead, he had to maneuver carefully through an obstacle course of etiquette. Before he could even enter the house, he was obliged to present his card at the front door. Then he had to decipher the reply: if he was informed that the lady he'd come to see was not at home, it might mean she really *wasn't* at home, or it might mean that she *was* at home but didn't want to see him. Which was it? His only choice was to wait for her invitation to call again. It might never come. But if it did come, the proper gentleman had to stall exactly two weeks before responding — no more, no less.

If he cleared the first hurdle and made it through to the actual meeting with the girl, he could expect not to be welcomed with refreshments, not to be accompanied to the door at his departure, and not to have anyone courteously make small

Rural folks once believed a sofa was an uncouth Turkish import, suggestive of harems. But things change . . .

The Origin of the X-Rated Greeting Card

For those lovers who had trouble composing their own verse in the late 1700s, there was a book called *The Young Man's Valentine Writer*, which offered all sorts of sentimental words for the taking. When, in the next century, postal rates went down, suitors found it more affordable to buy and send the new mass-produced cards. That practice allowed admirers the option of anonymity and with it came an air of intrigue. Post cards got racier. "The burgeoning number of obscene valentines caused several countries to ban the practice of exchanging cards," Panati's *Extraordinary Origins of Everyday Things* tells us. "In Chicago, for instance, in the late nineteenth century, the post

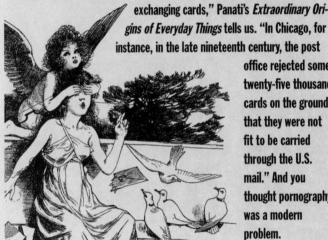

office rejected some twenty-five thousand cards on the ground that they were not fit to be carried through the U.S. mail." And you thought pornography was a modern problem.

talk while he fumbled with his coat. He was on his own. Those were the rules of courting etiquette — the rules that each young lady had learned from magazines such as the *Ladies' Home Journal* and that she knew would indicate to a gentleman (believe it or not) that she was interested in his attentions.

Perhaps the most telling clue available to a suitor at the time was whether the girl's parents stayed for his visit. Good etiquette mandated that the chaperons keep watch through the first encounter, but after that there was room for discretion. On later visits, the parents were allowed to step out for a walk if they approved of the suitor. If they didn't approve, they wouldn't leave, and that meant the courtship would soon be over. As merciless as it may seem to us now, that was the way of love back then. The nature of courtship took its form from the sofas on which it took place — straight-backed and uncomfortable.

From the Parlor to the Pontiac

All that changed with the popularization of the automobile in the early 1900s. Gentlemen could carry off their girls in fancy jalopies and escape the rigid etiquette of "calling" at home. But time with a sweetheart cost money — for Cokes, for movies, for dances, for gasoline — and men were the ones with the means to pay. With it they bought themselves the freedom to choose whom they pleased to court and the mobility to take their sweethearts where they wanted to go.

The trend took hold. By the 1920s, studies showed that young people considered staying at home "slow" compared with going out to a movie, motoring, or dancing in a neighboring town. In fact, of the young people polled in a 1929 study by sociologists Robert and Helen

Lynd in the midwestern village they called Middletown, half stayed home fewer than four nights a week. The automobile, it seemed, had become a rolling parlor. The back seat supplanted the sofa, and courtship opened up like a convertible top.

The modern style of dating made it easy for everyone to see who was going with whom; if you fell from favor, all your friends knew. To book a girl, men had to show they had the right goods — a good automobile, a good fraternity, good clothes, and good cash. Women, for their part, had to prove popularity to get a date. Breaking a rendezvous at the last minute showed that a woman was in demand. Boys put up with the humiliation so that they could eventually go out with the popular girls. One sociologist labeled the socializing pattern of the time "the rating and dating system."

Women's magazines like *Mademoiselle* and *Women's Home Companion* fueled dating anxiety by telling young women that it didn't matter how

In the "rating and dating system," women had to be perceived as popular, while men had to prove their worth in cars, clothes, and cash.

With the popularization of the automobile, true love was on a roll.

pretty or smart or well-dressed they were; all that mattered was that they be perceived as popular. To do this, the advice columnists suggested that incoming college freshmen get male friends from home to send telegrams, invitations, and letters, which could be shown around as proof of a girl's desirability. Competition for dates was so fierce at some colleges that the coeds had to make a pact not to date on certain weeknights, in order to have some time to study without losing points in the popularity race.

Who knows how bad the dating competition might have gotten if World War II hadn't intervened and changed the rules yet again. During the 1930s — the golden age for women on campus — there had been five men for every one woman at college. In the 1940s, with most able-bodied men off to war, there was only one man for every eight women. That left almost no chance for a coed to purposely overbook her social schedule no matter how popular she was. The pressures of wartime stretched money and frivolity to the breaking point. Cutting in at dances, once a commonplace occurrence, now became a severe insult. The one you were dancing with was the one you were dating full-time, the only one. "Going steady" became the big thing. Dreams reverted to the romantic notion of settling down at home, in the den, in front of the TV, on (guess what?) the sofa.

Yes, it had come back to that — which was, perhaps, to be expected. As anthropologist Margaret Mead once said, "Swings between Puritanism and license are as old as Methuselah." But, lucky for us, this time around the sofa had gotten a lot softer and more accommodating to our courtships. Instead of propelling us out the door as it had in the previous century, it seduced us further inward. The sixties would find the courtship trend swinging back again from the sofa to the bed. And by the seventies, we'd be curling up together for the long term in great numbers; childless cohabiting couples under 25 would rise eightfold. Suitors and girlfriends would become boyfriends and roommates. Courtships would become relationships.

And Back to the Bedroom

Certainly, young people still sat in restaurant booths, cuddled close in cars, and posed awkwardly on parents' sofas, but now women and men were freer to be risqué. The women's magazines, which had set the earlier rules, shifted their advice from the sedate to the seductive. In a 1990 article titled "How to Be a Great Date," *Cosmopolitan* suggested that women loosen up. "Don't be afraid to show a little leg or cleavage," the editors advised. "Order dessert — a lusty appetite is sexy; be touchy feely . . . brush up against him when entering a restaurant, let your knee lightly touch his in the cab."

The idea was to get him to crawl into bed with you. And, in fact, that's where most courtships were headed in the eighties and nineties — back to bundling in bed. After so many years of progress, we had progressed right back to where our Puritan forebears had started (replacing bundling boards, we should note, with prophylactics). And although we now engage in more sex than our Puritan forebears would have admitted to, we haven't changed courtship all that much. For a man can still come courting at the end of a hard week's work and find his sweetheart sitting up in bed, waiting to warm him beneath the covers. It's just that her parents won't be close by to tuck them in. ♥

"A lusty appetite is sexy," according to the editors of *Cosmo.*

For the Love of Lydia

In retrospect, it would be clear who was destined to win this turn-of-the-century courtship competition, but at the time anything seemed possible.

As a young woman, Lydia Auerbach stirred the hearts of many. She was born in 1887 in Buffalo, New York, to Otto Auerbach, who ran a school of music, and Lydia Auerbach, who raised young Lydia and her two siblings. Lydia was not especially different from other young women of her time. She was modest for the most part, believing that a girl's place was in the home and her duty was to help her mother. She enjoyed music and parties, and her main ambition was to find love. For a time, she had not one suitor, but three — Louis, Harry, and Stuart. Of the three, all would write love letters, two would stay friends with each other despite the competition, and only one would win her hand.

By saving the love letters she received in the early 1900s, Lydia saved for us a piece of romantic history. The letters, of course, are personal and detailed, but they also tell us something about courtship in a more general way: how phrases were turned to turn a heart; how distance created greater longing, not quickly crossed by car or train; and how words written almost a century ago still hold the power of passion for us today. Reading these letters, it is not hard to imagine oneself wooed as Lydia was by the words that say, over and over, what anyone would want to hear: you are wonderful; you are loved.

They begin in the fall of 1904, when a former classmate of Lydia's at Buffalo Central High School left for Cornell University and took with him her heart. His name was Louis W. Fehr. In later years, he

Theirs was a true-life tale of three eager bachelors, two broken hearts, and one abiding love.

The Valentine's Day Numbers

Number of Valentine's Day cards sent on a recent February 14: about 925 million

Increase from five years earlier: 150 million

Percentage of all valentines sent by women: 85 percent

Percentage of all valentines delivered by hand: roughly 50 percent

Estimated number of valentines sent to Elvis Presley in Graceland in a single recent year: 100

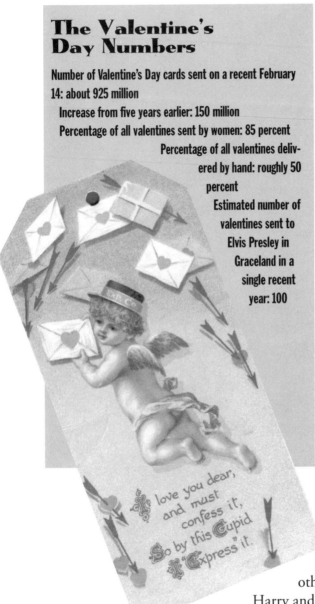

would pursue a successful career as a journalist, but in 1904 it was 17-year-old Lydia Auerbach who was his most passionate pursuit.

October 10, 1904
Dear Lydia —
Those moments that I spent with you at Goodrich's party were the most enchanting of my life —I was unconscious of anything, of anyone but you. How delighted I was to see you so radiant on Commencement night and how I envied your classmates and all Buffalonians who could be near you. I did not dare tell you then, but now with the miles between us, I cannot resist the impulse. If you could read my thoughts, you would know that of all the girls I have ever met you approach the closest to my ideal. Do me this undeserved favor and so make me your suitor forever. I am,
Your admirer,
Louis W. Fehr

Throughout that year and the next two, Louis's letters piled up. Lydia responded in kind, but now and then there were long gaps in her correspondence.

In 1906, two more suitors elbowed in on the affair. One was named J. Stuart Frazer, the other Harry Parsons. Their affection for Lydia put Harry and Stuart in the same boat.

Sunday 7/15/06
My dear Lydia — Can you guess where I am? At our cozy nook on Frenchman's bank. Harry Parsons came up the creek in the canoe with me this a.m. & I took him to our parlor in the woods. He seems a decent sort of chap. We have a crowd at Whitehall today (34 to dinner). But there are two lonesome fellows. Lydia, does it bother you to have me tell you

how I love you? It's not a crush, Lyd., but with me a hopeless case of strong and tender love growing deeper each day. I am very sorry that I cannot make you see it as I do. If it must be, Lydia, I can wait, but if the Lord wills I'll win your love yet. Must start and paddle my lonely way back. Well, I'll do as you say & try another ending but you know at the same time that I love you more than I can tell.

> *Bye-bye,*
> *Stuart*

And then there was Harry Parsons, the "decent chap" who had come up the creek in the canoe and befriended the love-struck Stuart. In his mid-20s, Harry was six years Lydia's senior. He hailed from Komoka, Ontario, and although he arrived last to the letter-writing game, he would come to be first in Lydia's heart. He wrote that he thought of her often, saying, "I soak in a very great deal of pleasure knowing you were there [at the concert] although we did not see each other."

Of the three, it was Louis who wrote most often, courting Lydia at least once a week. ("If I do not forget I will enclose a couple of blossoms I plucked especially for you. . . .") His love for her grew through their letters. Actual meetings were rare but precious; to Louis, they were the happiest times of his life. When they were not together, he tried to impress Lydia with his achievements at Cornell — his debating matches, his studies, his journalism leads. He could do it all, he told her, because he had her as his inspiration.

At times Louis was "wickedly jealous" of the other boys she dated and wanted to claim her for his own. But his studies came first; he strongly believed that a college man should not be engaged and had

The Dimple Device (Pat. Pend.)

Patent No. 560,351, dated May 19, 1896.

Be it known that I, Martin Goetze, a subject of the King of Prussia, Emperor of Germany . . . have invented new and useful Improvements Relating to Apparatus for the Production of Dimples on the Human Body, of which the following is a specification.

In order to make the body susceptible to the production of artistic dimples, it is necessary, as has been proved by numerous experiments, that the cellular tissues surrounding the spot where the dimple is to be produced should be made susceptible to its production by means of massage. This condition is fulfilled by the present process as well as by the apparatus by which the process is worked, and which is represented in an enlarged form in the accompanying drawing.

asked her to wait two more years until 1908, when he would complete his training. While Lydia waited, Louis continued to swear his devotion to her, but in a postscript there is a telling note: "I have mislaid those flowers."

Lydia, for her part, kept her options open. There were passionate encounters with her other two suitors. She tried to dismiss her indiscretions with regret and to save herself for Louis, but Stuart was determined to fight the current and win her devotion. One Wednesday evening, he sent this undated letter:

> My dear Lydia,
> . . . let me tell you that I am very sorry that I made you false to your "Prince Charming." You accuse me of betraying a trust you placed in me. Oh Lydia, if you but knew how I fought, and have fought many times, my own desires and passions because I knew that you wished it otherwise, you could not doubt my love. Girlie, I long to pour it out here but you have my promise . . . if you say two years, I am willing to be governed accordingly. While it seems a long time, I will be many times repaid, if I may win you, Sweetheart, in the end. (Don't take exception to that name this time.) God grant that I may be your Prince Charming. . . .
> Yours,
> Stuart

Clearly, Stuart, too, was jealous of the other fellows. His friend Harry was wanting Lydia for his own as well. But at least Harry had a sense his chances were better. Perhaps because of that, he took a more confident approach

Love Will Light the Way

In 1909, a bill was introduced in the Massachusetts state legislature that would compel all vehicles to carry lights at night. Freshman senator Dennis E. Farley, from the small western Massachusetts town of Erving, denounced it as an invasion of lovers' rights.

"Suppose a fellow wants to take his best girl out driving after his day's work," Farley argued. "What are you going to do? Make him carry a lighted lantern along with his girl?" In a senate speech, he hinted that this was a sinister plot by Bostonians to depopulate rural western Massachusetts. "In the name of horse discipline and human freedom," he told the senate, "I ask you to reject this abominable bill." Senate members shouted the bill down.

Two years later, however, after Farley had departed, the bill was overwhelmingly passed, with no (apparent) negative impact on the population.

in his missives to Lydia. Even before he had fully won her over, he described his feelings of power and well-being when he believed he had her at his side: "Oh! Dearie that world is surely more beautiful than ever. There is only one reason — you."

And sure enough, the approach worked. Harry's self-assurance and vision for the future won Lydia over. Tired of waiting for Louis to finish at Cornell, and unwilling to give in to Stuart's passion, Lydia accepted Harry's proposal of marriage. The excitement of the decision was tinged by an awareness of the disappointment that would come when she told the two runners-up of her engagement. Louis, at first, couldn't believe it.

January 5th, 1907
Dear Lydia, —
I have hoped that perhaps your engagement, like your sudden trip you told me of over the long distance telephone that Friday, was only a merciful falsehood to keep me from putting my neck beneath your feet — to save me the humiliation and yourself the pain of refusal, of what you suspected I would ask if I came. Drowning men grasp at straws and prolong their agony. If this is a delusion, take it away from me.
Sincerely,
Louis W. Fehr

But Lydia had made up her mind, and it was too late for Louis to do anything about it. It was too late as well for Stuart, who didn't get the news till three months later. He replied then in ink and tears.

April 10 — 07
My dear Lydia: —
You will never realize how your letter

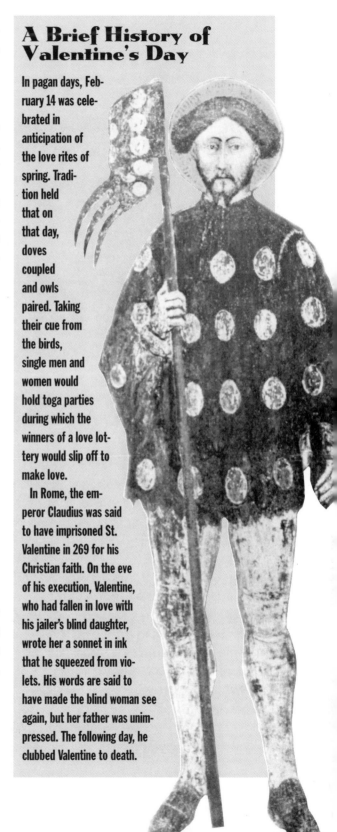

A Brief History of Valentine's Day

In pagan days, February 14 was celebrated in anticipation of the love rites of spring. Tradition held that on that day, doves coupled and owls paired. Taking their cue from the birds, single men and women would hold toga parties during which the winners of a love lottery would slip off to make love.

In Rome, the emperor Claudius was said to have imprisoned St. Valentine in 269 for his Christian faith. On the eve of his execution, Valentine, who had fallen in love with his jailer's blind daughter, wrote her a sonnet in ink that he squeezed from violets. His words are said to have made the blind woman see again, but her father was unimpressed. The following day, he clubbed Valentine to death.

Our Very Own (Well, Sort of) Love Story

Who has the time these days to court a lover when $200 will buy you a customized love story to order from California's Swan Publishing? All you need to do is fill out the order form, and a personalized version of one of five romance novels will be yours. Choose Lotto Love (Find Riches and Romance All in the Same Night!), Paradise Dream (The Hawaiian Adventure Romance), Our Love (The Californian Romance), or either of two other titles. Be sure to specify such details as your hero's hair color, nickname, or special song, or your heroine's favorite flowers. Note how they first met, what attracted them to each other, a special joke, or a secret "sign" that they share. Don't forget to describe their courtship (was it whirlwind, passionate, or long?) and their first kiss. Swan Publishing founder, Evelyn Brown, will plug the information into her computer, and — presto! — you (and more than 2,000 others) will have your very own personal story of love.

hurt, Lydia, and I hope you may never have reason for feeling quite as I do now. …That blot only shows how I feel.… No, I do not blame you. You did what was the fair thing under the circumstances but it is very, very hard to see all your dearest wishes and desires go to smash.

As ever,
Stuart

Neither Stuart nor Louis could let her go. She had brought out the poetry in their lives, and the letters did not end right away. With those two still wooing her, Harry sensed his engagement wasn't secure. Two years into it, he still sent letters like this:

Sept. 15 — 09
My Darling Girlie.
May God in his goodness give us hearts true and strong and may "right" win. If I lose you, you will be happier — but if I win you — ah! what sweetness! Such a sad truism — "man's love is of his life a part — tis woman's whole existence." How lucky a woman is!
Ever yours,
Harry

Lydia stayed true. Though she hadn't wanted to wait two years for Louis, she stayed engaged for three to Harry. And so at last, in 1910, Harry Leslie Parsons and Lydia Marie Auerbach passed from courtship to marriage. They lived first in Vancouver, then in Toronto, and later in New York City.

"How people must love each other," Harry had written to Lydia before they married, "after they are actually husband and wife living under the same roof — partaking of each other's joys and sorrows, sleeping in each other's arms!" But the idyllic picture he had imagined did not come true right away in the reality of daily marriage. The times of separation and reunion continued, and prewedding jealousies rekindled now and then. Harry learned that courtship shouldn't end with the wedding — that Lydia still wanted him to pour his heart out on the page. And years into the marriage, he was still writing his wife love letters.

Dearest Dearest Darling ——

. . . I just want to love and love and love you Dear — for hours! I want to claim you completely and just smother you with kisses and loving embraces.

Your wonderful, wonderful love has helped me win out in spite of severe handicaps. My whole life is yours to do with as you will — everything Dear. I'm your devoted slave honey — and you are my very soul — It's more than a passing burst of passion Dear — (that is so sweet tho too) — it is the loveliest most beautiful realization that can come to a man to know that he has a beautiful woman who loves him as fondly as you love me and to know that my love is entirely yours and that

Terms of Endearment

There are pet names you love and pet names you hate. Here's how 1,000 people surveyed by a market research firm for Korbel Champagne ranked their favorites:

1. Honey
2. His/Her name
3. Baby
4. Sweetheart
5. Dear
6. Lover
7. Darling
8. Sugar
9. Pumpkin/Angel (tied)
10. Precious/Beautiful (tied)

"My little chickadee" didn't make the Top 10.

First You Have to Find a Rain Barrel

On the first day of spring, shout into a rain barrel that stands at the corner of the house. According to tradition, if you hear an echo, you will marry the first unmarried man who comes around the corner.

you reciprocate as fully as I do. . . . I haven't seen a single girl for whom I'd barter your little toe! And the lovely part of it all is that it has always been so from the day I met you. So completely and rapturously yours.
 Lovingly
 Harry

In 1918, Lydia gave birth to a daughter, Doris, and in 1929 to another they named Eleanor. Later they went to live in St. Petersburg, Florida. Over the next four decades, their marriage eventually became what Harry had always wanted: "The mother sitting at the table — the father sitting beside her — keeping his old habit of liking to have her close to him even though he was falling into the middle aged comforts of an easy chair and a newspaper." But it couldn't last forever. In 1970, that sweet domestic scene came to an end with Harry's death.

After two years of mourning, Lydia, age 85, tracked down Stuart, her long-ago sweetheart, at his daughter's house in Howell, Michigan. Not only was he still alive, but he remembered her well. He sent this reply:

My dear Lydia:
 I am the John Stuart Frazer for whom you have been looking. . . . We are nicely situated here [at our daughter's]. . . . Mabel's health has been such for the past two years that I had to have help in taking care of her. . . . Next month we will

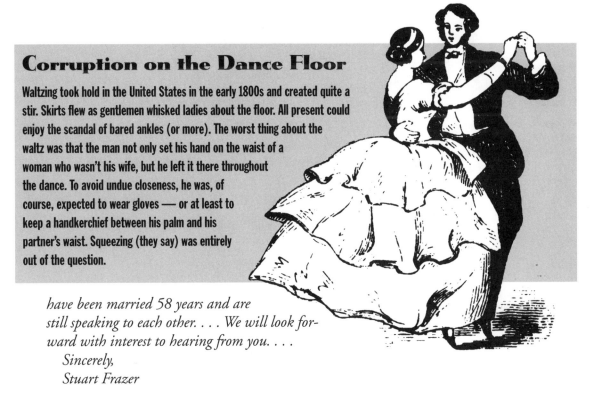

Corruption on the Dance Floor

Waltzing took hold in the United States in the early 1800s and created quite a stir. Skirts flew as gentlemen whisked ladies about the floor. All present could enjoy the scandal of bared ankles (or more). The worst thing about the waltz was that the man not only set his hand on the waist of a woman who wasn't his wife, but he left it there throughout the dance. To avoid undue closeness, he was, of course, expected to wear gloves — or at least to keep a handkerchief between his palm and his partner's waist. Squeezing (they say) was entirely out of the question.

have been married 58 years and are
still speaking to each other. . . . We will look for-
ward with interest to hearing from you. . . .
    Sincerely,
    Stuart Frazer

They wrote now and then, exchanged Christmas cards. Then one day a letter came from Stuart's daughter, notifying Lydia of Stuart's death. He was "very frail and very tired," his daughter wrote, "and went into a coma and just quietly slept away." Until the end, she said, he had eagerly awaited Lydia's letters.

In 1976, the 89-year-old Lydia tried to find her other long-lost love, Louis. She wrote to the school from which he had written to her so many dozens and dozens of treasured love letters. Cornell University responded with the sad news that Louis Fehr had died 19 years earlier. A nephew filled in a few more details for Lydia. Louis had been a successful political writer for the *New York Times,* but his last years had been sad. "His marriage was very unhappy," the nephew wrote. "Uncle Louis married a Jewish woman who was a talented pianist, but not much else." He had made Lydia wait for him for two years and in the end had waited all his life for a love like hers.

So it is, in the end, that we all make our deals with life: some find fame; some find love. As for Lydia Marie Auerbach Parsons, she died in 1985 in St. Petersburg, Florida, at the age of 97. She left behind the cardboard boxes containing the carefully creased letters of her three suitors — the three who, for a time, had all believed what the one had written: "there is no world but you." ♥

The Engage

Popping the question,

buying the dress, choosing the ring — all of these are covered here. If you've been engaged, you will have your own stories to tell. If you're still waiting, you can read ours. In either case, you will realize from the forthright material that follows that engagement is not always (in fact, is seldom) the purely blissful and idyllic state that it is so often imagined to be. Phones will be ringing, it's true. People will be asking to see your ring, yes. Some may even see in you something they hadn't seen before. So what if you have to deal with all those invitations, all those decisions, all those disputes between the bride's family and the groom's, all the money to be spent — it's all in the name of eternal love, right?

ment

"Will You . . .
Will You . . .
Pass the Butter?"

Some helpful hints about popping the — you know — the question.

When Aunt Lois asks pointedly, "Any news, dear?" she's not referring to the Middle East peace talks. And when your father starts wondering aloud about a beau's "intentions," he's not musing about whether or not he's going to run for Congress. And so, the pressure's on. Will he or won't he ask? Will you or won't you accept? And if you do, what will everyone say then?
— The Engaged Woman's Survival Guide

You'll do well to say something that has a nice ring to it.

No matter what they say, do not despair. Love comes to those who wait. If you're not engaged, it's not too late. Every day eight Americans over the age of 65 marry for the first time. If

Leap Year Courtship

"Say the word, Leopold and make me the happiest girl in the world!"

A woman's opportunity comes just once every four years, so she must be ready to make the leap when he won't.

you are engaged and feel it will never end, have faith, too. Octavio Guillen and Adriana Martinez of Mexico City stayed engaged for 67 years (the longest on record, according to Guinness) before they finally took the plunge at the age of 82. Don't give up yet on the whole business of marriage, for remember, as Mae West said, "a man in the house is worth two in the street." Sooner or later, he will get up the courage to pop that question.

Will You . . . . Will You . . . Watch the Red Sox with Me Tonight?

The first thing to remember when asking the question is what the question is. (Crib notes not advised.) Four little words that, when said in the right order and followed by a certain three-letter word, will add up to eternity (or as close as you're likely to come these days).

Once you've got the question straight, you may wonder whose job it is to ask. The fact is that 92 percent of all marriage proposals are still made by men, so if you're a guy (and you're not Keanu Reeves or Brad Pitt, who have scores of women proposing to them each year), you'll likely be waiting a long, long time — up to four years, in fact — for the woman to ask.

Fortunately, tradition has it that every leap year unwed women can pose the question to negligent swains. That custom got its start with Julius Caesar, who rearranged the calendar in 46 B.C. to tack on an extra day every fourth year. About seven centuries later, according to legend, a liberated nun named St. Bridget got after St. Patrick to stir up support for each woman to have a chance to choose the man of her dreams. St. Patrick decreed that any man refusing a leap year proposal should pay the rejected damsel a silk gown and a kiss. (Not a bad form of rejection considering you'd at least get a new outfit out of it.)

But what if it's not leap year when you finally get up the courage to ask him to marry you? What if it's the mid-1800s and you're an

18-year-old who's just been crowned the queen of the United Kingdom and told to produce an heir to the throne when you haven't even a spouse in sight? Would you do as Queen Victoria did — summon your German cousin Prince Albert and tell him to marry you? Well, whether you would or would not, Victoria did, and Albert consented. Later she confessed in a letter that the reason she'd taken the initiative was that she knew Albert would "never have presumed to take such a liberty as to propose to the queen of England."

How a Girl Gets Her Way

But that, of course, was a special case in point. Most women with less authority than the queen of England have settled on making their preferences known in more subtle or underhanded ways. Years ago, the young women at Wellesley College in Massachusetts used to take their sweethearts to Tupelo Point at Lake Waban. If the suitor didn't propose after three excursions, tradition permitted the woman to push him into the lake. In one form or another, he'd end up testing the waters of love.

Those who prefer to avoid such extremes can do nothing but

"Look, Sweetie, one way or another you *will* take the plunge."

wait. Give the guy time. He may not realize what he's up against. He may be blocking the question. He may think getting engaged is as easy as getting football tickets to a college game. Or he may simply fear rejection. After all, if it took Crown Prince Naruhito — a guy on deck for the throne of Japan — three proposals to get a commoner to accept, what sort of chance does the average Joe have? If even Clark Gable and Jimmy Stewart could be turned down by the same woman (Anita Colby, the nation's first supermodel), then why not just call the whole thing off and resolve to drive around in the free state of eternal bachelor bliss?

Because a man is eventually bound to get bored. Even Hugh Hefner, the king of *Playboy* magazine, finally did. At age 61 (having been married once before and divorced), he proposed in a traditional way to *Playboy* model Kimberley Conrad. She had just beat him at foosball and was standing beside him at the wishing well outside his house when he asked, "Would you like to marry me?" She said yes and reminded him that the last time they had been at the well she had tossed a coin in and made a wish. "This is what I wished for," she said. And he replied, "This is what I wished for, too." A year later, the wedding ceremony took place at that very well.

Dear Diary: Never Mind . . .

In 19th-century Russia, it was the custom for a betrothed couple to read each other's diaries before they married. That way there'd be no secrets between them. In the case of author Leo Tolstoy and his future wife, Sonya, the exchange of diaries created great turmoil four days before their wedding, and then throughout their marriage. While 18-year-old Sonya's diaries disclosed only a sheltered life, 34-year-old Tolstoy's were filled with stories of gambling, drunken orgies, and homosexual longings, as well as details of his ongoing emotional affair with a peasant woman who had given birth to his illegitimate son. Which just goes to show that if you must indulge in excesses, it may be best not to take notes.

Tolstoy's diary proved he was a novel lover.

Revving Up for Romance

So you see, the freewheeling days of singledom eventually end in matrimony for even the wildest of wanderers. And when they do, they will most likely end in a practical way, with a man and a woman joining together because they meet each other's needs. So says motivation psychologist Dr. Ernest Dichter in an *Esquire* report: "Although men ogle convertibles (which symbolize freedom, romance, a touch of danger),

Although men ogle convertibles, they marry sedans.

they marry sedans (practical, useful, and safe)." So sooner or later you, too, will settle into that perfect sedan-tarry state, and when you choose to, you may wonder what's the best approach.

For years, men have used their wits to come up with new and stunning ways to propose — the theory being that if you go to enough trouble and expense, your girlfriend will be either sufficiently flattered or sufficiently embarrassed to say yes. As a result, a whole proposal industry has grown up to supply men with creative opportunities. Several years ago, in Taylor, Michigan, a man dressed as a knight in shining armor delivered proposals on a white stal-

Widowed Before They Wed

In China, engagement traditionally was such a serious event that the wedding ceremony had to be held even if the bridegroom died beforehand. In such a case, the poor bride was obligated to proceed straight from engagement to widowhood.

lion to those "damsels" who would hear him out. In Naples Island, California, entrepreneurs still paddle couples in a gondola through the canals (hoping, of course, that they have no water phobias). And across the country, newspapers offer personal columns and full-page ads for lovers wanting to wed (the hope being that your intended doesn't line her bird's cage with your newspaper testament of love). Several years ago, in fact, a Swedish man paid more than $16,000 for a marriage proposal ad that included his phone number. Although he got several calls from interested women, none came from the one for whom the ad was intended. It turned out she hadn't even received her newspaper that morning. (Don't you hate it when that happens?)

If at First You Don't Succeed . . .

But that rejection, at least, was only a matter of poor delivery, not a matter of personal distaste. Nowhere near as bad as what happened to Samuel Clemens (a.k.a. Mark Twain). Intent on marrying Olivia Langdon, Clemens knew that she wouldn't accept unless her father did, too. Unfortunately for the rough-edged Clemens, Mr. Langdon was a high-class New Yorker who required references. What was worse was that the letters Clemens supplied from his friends weren't at all in his favor. In fact, every one gave the author a thumb's-down review, and two even predicted that he would die a drunkard. Lucky for him, however, Mr. Langdon didn't dismiss him out of hand. "Haven't you a friend in the world?" he asked the prospective groom.

"Apparently not," said Clemens.

"Take the girl," Langdon conceded. "I know you better than they do."

As it turned out, Langdon was right. Clemens

When Olivia's dad took a chance on Mark, he hoped his daughter's heart wouldn't be broken in Twain.

yes!

made not only an affectionate and loyal husband but quite a good author to boot.

The point here is to persevere. Do what works for you. If you can't get good references, try straight-out sentiment. Rent a limousine, get down on one knee (provided you're not driving), and tell her you love her. Al Joyner won over the fastest woman in the world that way. "I think you're the most beautiful, straightforward woman in the world," Al said, "and I want to ask you, will you marry me?" Florence Griffith didn't say yes right off, but she did cry for forty-five minutes (usually a good sign). He handed her a box with a two-carat diamond engagement ring in it, and she managed a thank-you. The next day, they were at a pizza parlor arcade when Flo's seven-year-old niece traded in her game tickets for rubber letters that spelled out "yes." The girl handed the letters to Florence. Florence told Al to close his eyes and open his hands, then gave him her answer that way. Which was nice.

Try Investing in Real Estate

Things work out. And if it seems they're not going to at first, you can always do something drastic like buy a house. A guy named Bill Clinton tried that to win the woman of his dreams — a woman named Hillary Rodham, who'd been teaching criminal law and trial advocacy at the University of Arkansas while he'd been running for Congress. She had come home for a break. Bill picked her up at the airport and sprung it on her, saying, "I bought the house you like, so you better marry me

Five Signs of an Approaching Wedding

1. A cow lows during the night.
2. A mockingbird flies over the house.
3. A white dove comes near the house.
4. A spider dangles her web down from the ceiling, and you bounce her on her thread.
5. A chicken comes into the house with a piece of straw in its beak and lays it down.

Had *The Volga Boatman* (1926) been a talkie, everyone might have known the stars' little secret.

because I can't live in it by myself." That brick house in Fayetteville she liked so much served well as the setting for their wedding ceremony on October 11, 1975.

You get the picture. Hit when the mood strikes. Do what feels right. Movie stars Demi Moore and Bruce Willis had been attending a boxing match (not the most romantic of settings) in Las Vegas when he turned to her at the gambling tables of the Golden Nugget Hotel and said, "We could get married, you know." They'd only been together four months, but the time was ripe. Within a few hours, they'd picked up a license from an around-the-clock marriage bureau (they have those in Las Vegas) and returned to their hotel. Demi grabbed flowers from an urn in the hotel lobby, and they went upstairs to their room to be married by a minister waiting there.

Why Wait?

Spontaneity is romantic, and

The Groom Made a Mess

The stag party, it's believed, began with the soldiers of ancient Sparta, who feasted with the groom on the night before his wedding. It was called, appropriately, "the men's mess," and was meant to confirm loyalty among the men despite the impending intrusion of a feminine being in the groom's life.

more people than you'd think jump right into marriage that way. They say they just know from the first moment they set eyes on each other. And maybe they do. Actor Michael Douglas and filmmaker Diandra Luker got married two months after they met at a party over the hors d'oeuvres table. They lived on opposite ends of the country, but he called from California to Washington every day for a week until she agreed to visit him for a weekend in California. She told her roommate that if her mother called, the roommate should say that Diandra was at the library. That ruse might have worked for a weekend, but Diandra stayed at Michael's California apartment for two weeks. "I don't think your mother believes me," her roommate told her. Diandra, of course, was in love. Michael was, too. One day in the car he said out of the blue, "I think we should get married. Will you marry me? I love you and can't live without you." So they married.

Read My Lips

The proposal can come at any time. Sometimes, when it's least expected. None of the people watching Cecil B. De Mille's silent film *The Volga Boatman* in 1926 knew that Boyd, the actor playing Feodor, had proposed real-life marriage to Elinor during the scene when he was awaiting execution. But he had, and she'd accepted.

In the end, proposing marriage is always worth the risk. For in the wise words of the great Greek philosopher Socrates, you can't go wrong. "By all means marry," Socrates advised. "If you get a good wife, you'll become happy; if you get a bad one, you'll become a philosopher." ♥

Could it have been a marital issue that made Socrates so philosophical about taking the hemlock?

The Circle of Love

Anything is possible, as long as you remember the ring.

Engagement rings have been the thing since ancient times, when a piece of gold or silver was broken, and the man and woman each kept half until they could be joined in marriage.

Giving an engagement ring was common throughout the Middle Ages as well — in England, in southern Europe, and elsewhere. In the United States, the custom didn't catch on until the 1840s. At that time, rings were given by both the man and the woman as a public statement of commitment. So much symbolic value was placed on the token that people believed if the engagement ring was lost or damaged, bad luck would come to the couple. Likewise, if another woman tried on the ring, the bride's future happiness would be at stake. The best bet was to keep the ring firmly in place on the engaged woman's hand.

Although the fiancée's birthstone is said to be a lucky one for an engagement ring, the diamond is still the stone of choice. This is nothing new. Early Italians, believing that the diamond was created in the fire of love, cherished it. But diamonds didn't become popular in the United States until exploitation of South African diamond deposits made them more affordable in the 19th century.

By the 1990s, men in this country would spend close to $3 billion a year to get engaged. And although many a man might like to buy the biggest rock around to prove his love, he is forced to settle for what he can afford. Bridal experts suggest that a man spend no more than two months' salary on a diamond ring, so that the symbol of eternal love does not sink him in eternal debt. Those more fortunate or more famous can afford to be a little flashier.

The king of rock 'n' roll, for example, could easily afford to give up the 11 1/2-carat ring on his hand when he decided to marry for the second time. He presented it to 20-year-old Ginger Alden on the day he decided to marry her, though he'd known her for only nine weeks.

What happened was this: the 42-year-old Elvis had looked up the best proposal date in *Cheiro's Book of Numbers* and found it was that very day. Having no time to buy an appropriate engagement ring, he had the stone from his own ring reset for his love. Then he sat the unsuspecting Ginger in his favorite place — the reading chair beside his bathroom throne — kneeled before her, and declared his love.

The scene was so overwhelmingly romantic (according to the *Elvis* account by Albert Goldman) — with the beautiful ring, the flowery speech, the glistening bathroom fixtures — that all Ginger could say was "Yes."

Tragically, the wedding did not take place, because only weeks later, Elvis died of a heart attack in that very bathroom. But who knows how many others were inspired by the King of Rock's passion to offer their own proposals — along with the perfect ring. ♥

How do I love thee? Let me count the carats.

109

The Dress

In the face of impending marriage, it is of the utmost importance that you keep your priorities in order . . .

So now you're engaged. Never again will you be entitled to call together all the significant people in your life and expect them to show up and sit politely for an hour or so while you and your sweetheart expound on how much you will love each other forever and ever, amen. But that's what you're about to do, and you darn well better look good for the occasion, because the next time this many people will pay this much attention to you is at your funeral, and God knows you won't have much choice in the matter of appearances *then*.

You've no doubt realized that nothing in your closet will do. And even if it did do, you wouldn't want it to, because the whole idea here is that you are starting a fresh, new life. White, of course, speaks volumes.

But what it says depends on where and when you live. In Asia, white was traditionally worn at a wedding to symbolize mourning — the bride was, after all, departing from her birth family. In biblical days, white would've meant that a bride was unchaste; blue was the preferred color of purity. In the second quarter of the 19th century, white worn by a country bride indicated that she was simply impractical.

The white wedding dress has come and gone as often

What are you trying to say with that white wedding dress? Are you starting fresh? Or could it be a symbol of mourning, impurity, or impracticality?

In the "closet marriages" of 19th-century widows, all was laid bare.

as the shifting tides of hemlines. It washed in first with Anne of Brittany, when in 1499 she wed Louis XII of France. Then it washed out. It washed back in again in the late 18th century, when the best day dresses of most country women were of white spun linen. White made sense during that period because women could grow the flax, spin it, weave it, cut it, and sew their own wedding dresses from it. The beauty of what a woman wore on her wedding day — a dress of skillfully hatcheled flax — revealed a crafted hand, a patient soul.

The Naked Facts

Widows at that time weren't given that chance; they were expected to marry naked. In those days, everything in a widow's possession — even the linens and wedding outfit of her own making — was considered by law to belong to her dead husband. To show that she brought none of his baggage to her second marriage, the second-time bride stood naked beside the road for the wedding ceremony, wearing only the cloak of dusk.

Around the turn of the

Closer My Love to Thee

In the 18th and early 19th centuries, state law and church rules required that the betrothal be made official through a notice posted on the door of a meetinghouse and by an announcement made from the pulpit. Later, in the mid-1800s in Massachusetts, a man could make his intentions known simply by switching his seat in church from his family's pew to his sweetheart's.

19th century, social customs lightened up enough to permit a widowed bride to hide naked in a closet for the wedding, with just her arm and hand exposed through a diamond-shaped hole in the door. It was called, for obvious reasons, a closet marriage.

If there was no closet available, someone stretched a blanket from the chimney to a corner, and the bride stood behind it. Her attendants stripped off her clothes and tossed them into the room. She stuck her bare arm through a small opening in the blanket and clasped her husband's hand in hers. After the final vows had been spoken (hers, we assume, sounding somewhat muffled), the kind groom stuffed a wedding outfit behind the blanket. Following some hurried fumbling, she emerged pristinely attired to accept the good wishes of the guests.

Times, thank goodness, have changed, and so too have fashions. In the early 1800s, the dress an engaged woman chose for her wedding had to be more practical, even if she lived in the "civilized" Northeast. These were pioneers, after all; a dress put on for just one day would be a ridiculous extravagance. What they wanted was something fancy, but something cheap, too, something that they could stitch together themselves and that would pack well for the trip west. A yellow or red cotton or wool dress, which after the wedding could serve through

Queen for a day? Take your cue from Victoria: white dress, white veil, and orange blossoms.

114

the hard-working days that followed, would be good. Versatility was the key.

A Bolt Out of the Blue

As the second quarter of the 19th century rolled in, textile mills were sprouting up around New England, and manufactured material was easier to come by. If the prospective bride lived anywhere near a city, she could ask her father to buy some colored cloth on his next trip to town. Besides seaming and hemming her dress, the hardest thing a woman had to do was to choose the hue that suited her best.

All sorts of colors were popular at the time. But in February 1840, a ceremony took place that would influence wedding fashion for generations to come. Queen Victoria married her cousin Prince Albert, and the flair with which she did it made her wedding the social event of the century. She was 20 years old — old enough, as they say, to know better and young enough not to care. Historically, virtually all European queens (except Anne of Britanny) had worn colorful but cumbersome ermine and velvet robes with elaborate (some would say gaudy) brocades. Victoria couldn't bear the thought. "Much better white," she declared in her diary two months before the wedding. The palace courtiers harrumphed, then acquiesced. What the queen wanted, the queen got — white it would be.

From March to November, 200 craftspeople bent to the task of completing the intricate lace needed for the yards of material that made up Victoria's gown. Fashion columnists in Britain had formerly pooh-poohed white as plain and old-fashioned; now they and thousands of publications

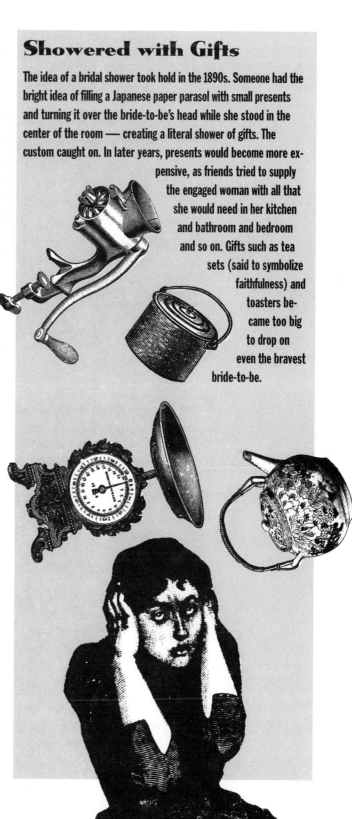

Showered with Gifts

The idea of a bridal shower took hold in the 1890s. Someone had the bright idea of filling a Japanese paper parasol with small presents and turning it over the bride-to-be's head while she stood in the center of the room — creating a literal shower of gifts. The custom caught on. In later years, presents would become more expensive, as friends tried to supply the engaged woman with all that she would need in her kitchen and bathroom and bedroom and so on. Gifts such as tea sets (said to symbolize faithfulness) and toasters became too big to drop on even the bravest bride-to-be.

I Wouldn't Marry You for a Million Dollars

At the turn of the century, actress and singer Lillian Russell turned down "Diamond Jim" Brady's offer of marriage, even though he had just deposited $1 million cash in her lap. She declined, she said, because marriage would ruin a beautiful friendship. Would you marry someone you didn't love for a million dollars? Twenty-three percent of the men and 21 percent of the women polled by *Psychology Today* magazine in a recent survey said that they would.

Diamond Jim couldn't get Lil for a cool mil.

across America applauded the fine elegance of the queen's choice. Have you heard?! White! Absolutely stunning! Simply splendid! Word went out, and women in all corners of Britain and America took note.

The Wedding of the Century

On Monday, the 10th of February, just after midday, Victoria strode down the aisle dressed in a white satin gown. A deep flounce of Honiton lace heightened the effect. Her Turkish diamond necklace and earrings shone. The sapphire brooch that Albert had given her sparkled on her bosom. Orange blossoms wreathed her hair. Behind her, a dozen trainbearers, dressed in matching white satin, carried her white satin court train trimmed with orange blossom sprays. That day, before the world's very eyes, Queen Victoria achieved what all brides had sought: an exalted state of stunning grace.

What the queen wore, the women of the world would wear, too (at least in some watered-down imitation). Thereafter, almost every bride in America tried to follow suit, down to the last detail. Advice books, such as *The Art of Good Behavior*, passed along instructions for the uniform: "The bride is usually dressed in pure white — she wears a white veil, and her head is crowned with a wreath . . . orange blossoms are preferred. She should wear no ornaments but such as her intended husband or her father may present her for the occasion — certainly no gift, if any such were retained, of any former sweetheart."

That was it. People in later years would forget that white hadn't always been in vogue. They would come to believe that it

I'm Pulling My Hair Out Over You

In Yugoslavia, custom once had it that the bridegroom was shaved in public before his wedding. The onlookers then gathered every hair of his beard, wrapped it in a towel, and sent it to his bride.

In the old days of Ireland, the custom was for the man to present a woven bracelet of human hair to his intended. The circle, of course, represented unending union.

had been the original bridal fashion, symbolizing purity. Just like Christmas, they would think, it wouldn't be right if it weren't white.

In the high excitement of the day, what eager brides and etiquette-conscious matrons failed to realize was that Victoria had looked so absolutely stunning because she had been original; she had selected the details and decked herself in the clothes that most suited her. Those who mimicked her style couldn't help but fail in re-creating her

There was sew much pressure for the bride-to-be to prove she could cut it.

118

uniqueness. Still, the style stuck. The queen — as queens often do — had set the fashion for the common folk, and originality became business as usual.

Following the Dotted Line of Fashion

A market grew to meet the demand for the latest wedding styles. In the 1850s, *Peterson's Magazine* and *Godey's Lady's Book* provided miniature diagrammed patterns that diligent brides-to-be could cut and sew at home. Within two decades, the McCall Pattern Company and tailors such as Ebenezer Butterick offered full-size patterns and made-to-order completed dresses. As the Industrial Revolution continued, more affordable material became available even in the American West. Soon, no matter how remote the outpost, a prospective bride could order her choice of material (even silk), specify the dips and frills and sashes she wanted, and have the completed gown sent to her distant ranch. Or if an uncle happened to pass through a well-stocked town while out on a cattle drive, so much the better — he could pick up his niece's stylish gown and carry it home.

There were those, of course, who at the end of the 19th century still chose to be practical, to deviate from the traditional white gown with more wearable colors like navy blue, green, or brown shaped into a two- or three-piece suit of satin, silk, or velvet. The choice carried great weight in the neighborhood, because family and friends knew that what an engaged woman chose to wear would foreshadow the way she would later act as a wife. Would she be practical or pretty? Could she be both?

Preparing for the wedding was like readying for a trip into the unknown. The wedding dress and the bride's trousseau had to be as carefully set as a compass pointed toward new territory. As Dr. Mary Roberts wrote in her 1912 book *Why Women Are So,* "A trousseau was as essential to the prospective bride as an outfit to the explorer of Arctic or tropical wilds . . . who knew what might be needed and yet unattainable in the great adventure upon which she was about to embark!"

To prepare the trousseau, a prospective bride spent the final days of her engagement stitching linens and clothing. She sewed and shopped, packed and cleaned, sewed and

Whether it's for the trousseau or for exploring the Arctic, the right outfit is essential.

packed some more. There was no time to spare. The process became her transition into wifehood, and she certainly wanted to come out of it looking her absolute best.

The Battle for the Best Fit

A century later, some of us may think that we modern women have moved beyond that. Clearly, we've become more cultured through our careers and our educations and have advanced to new levels of sophistication that (sometimes) diminish our concern for appearances. But the wedding dress is still a big deal. Big enough, in fact, to keep numerous bridal magazines thick with ads. And big enough to create a stampede several times a year at the Filene's Basement Wedding Dress Sale. You may have heard of it. It's the dress sale that has become, in effect, the modern-day passage to wifedom; a rough and tumble ritual that happens in the spring beneath the streets of Boston.

Each year on the single day of the sale, hundreds of prospective brides from around the country descend on the department store. Within 40 seconds of the store's opening, they have scavenged all 800 dresses off the racks. Without a modicum of modesty, the brides-to-be strip to their underwear in the middle of the store, tug on white gowns, and elbow in at the mirrors. They grunt at what they see, then tear out of the gowns. Zippers get stripped, hems get soiled, lace gets torn. But the dresses at Filene's that day are so cheap — $249 marked down from as high as $3,000 — that no one cares about the later cost of alterations and cleaning. The object is simply to find the dress of one's dreams — the one that will make a woman appear as stately as Queen Victoria, the perfect bride.

To the uninitiated, each dress may look like all the others: white, off-white, white. But each woman has in mind the exact specifications of the perfect dress: sleeves to here, neck to here; feminine but not frilly, simple but not plain. The dress is so crucial that some women will track it down before they've found a fiancé (or boyfriend, for that matter). The man can come later; it's the dress that counts. The dress that alone will transform a woman when she wears it down the aisle. The dress that will make her feel that the curtains have opened, her beauty has shone, and her life has begun and will continue happily ever after.

We should know better by now. We should have pulled ourselves out of the dank basement of barbarity where a dress defines our beauty. But, no, wait! There's the dress. That's it! The dress! Hey, I saw it first — back off! It's mine!

And so, at the end of the day, the floor of Filene's Basement is littered with crushed rejects. The fittest of our species has emerged with the best fit. She has survived the rite of passage that entitles her to continue in an exalted state to her wedding day. That singular day of elegance. That day when we think it best that you not mention what you've seen here today. Now if you'd all be seated, here comes the bride . . . Would you look at that dress! ♥

"Back off that wedding dress, girl — that symbol of feminine charm is mine!"

The Wedding

Weddings

Weddings have become such a big business these days (Americans spend $15 billion on them annually) that the "industry" is almost as bad as big-league baseball. In the midst of all that exchanging of money, sometimes it seems we've lost the heart of the game. Spectators are distracted by the pageantry, and even the brides and grooms become dazed. We at *The Old Farmer's Almanac* feel that it is time to get back to basics. Consider this our little chalk talk before the game. In the following pages, we will walk you through the worst of wedding day disasters (so your big day will seem fine, no matter what happens); bone up on superstition; deconstruct the wedding in a blow-by-blow diagram; and send you off with the greatest wedding strategies of all time. Now go out there and knock 'em dead!

The Deconstruction of a Wedding

What's what and why.

Best Man

Bridesmen or "Bride-knights"

The Bridegroom

The Wedding Ring

The Veil

Why do people throw rice at the bridal couple? Why does the wedding party include bridesmaids? Why does the bride wear a veil? And why is the groom called a groom? Weddings have become such complicated affairs that we figured you might need an illustrated guide to make sense of it all.

Flowergirls

The Wedding Cake

Bridesmaids

Rice

The Tying of Shoes

RICE
100 LBS

RACING

JUST MARRIED!

4 RENT

Bridesmen or "Bride-knights"

During the days of the Anglo-Saxons, a man needed help to capture the woman of his choosing. He typically enlisted his friends, the bridesmen, for assistance. The duty of the "knights" was to get the bride to the church on time and keep the hostile family members at bay until the ceremony was completed. These days the bridesmen show the family to their seats.

Best Man

The man with the quickest sword around 200 A.D. was the groom's right-hand man. He not only aided in the capture of the bride-to-be but also stood guard through the ceremony and often through the wedding night. Nowadays, the best man has to be quick on the draw with the ring and the toast — no weapons training required.

The Wedding Ring

Wedding rings date back at least as far as the Egyptians, who used the circle in their hieroglyphics to represent eternity. Scholars later suggested that fetter symbolism might have been implied as well. Wedding rings have been made of everything from gold and wood to iron, leather, silver, and grass, with the most common being a plain band of gold. The ring is worn on the third finger of the left hand, because the Greeks maintained that a "vein of love" ran from that finger straight to the heart. More practically speaking, that finger is protected by the other fingers around it and is little used, so a ring worn there will not wear out quickly. The early Hebrews wore their wedding rings on the index finger, and the people of India use the thumb.

The Wedding Cake

Wedding cakes have been around since ancient Roman times — but in those days, they were called "bride cakes" and were made of grain and salt; the crumbs were thrown at the bride. During the American Civil War, two kinds of cake were served at the wedding: a white cake for the bride and a dark fruitcake for the groom. If the bride didn't cut the first piece of cake, folklore proclaimed that she would be without child. What's more, she had to save at least a crumb of cake to share with her husband on their first anniversary if they hoped to have a long and lucky life together.

Rice

Guests have thrown rice at wedding couples since the 1870s, hoping to encourage fruitful unions. Long before that, the Greeks threw grain, fruit, and sweetmeats; the Hebrews threw cake; and others threw petals or birdseed or wheat. Single women eager to speed the day of their own weddings often scrambled to catch the falling grains of wheat, much as we do today with the tossed bouquet.

The Tying of Shoes

In the 18th and 19th centuries, satin slippers were thrown at the carriage as the couple drove off. If a slipper landed on top, the newlyweds could count on eternal good luck. Old shoes are now tied to the couple's getaway car to aid fertility. (In ancient times, the foot was considered a phallic symbol, and the shoe was said to hold the owner's essence.)

The Bridegroom

In many cultures, the newly married man was supposed to wait on the table of his bride on her wedding day. Since a menial hand was called a groom, it made sense that the husband would be called the "bride's groom" (at least for the day).

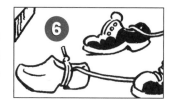

Flowergirls

The duty of flowergirls originally was not merely to scatter petals or carry the bride's train, but something more essential — to ward off demonic forces. The bride was thought to be especially vulnerable on her wedding day, and the power of the girls' virginity was thought to be especially strong as a shield against the Devil.

The Veil

During the early days of the Anglo-Saxons, the heads of both the bride and the groom were covered with a "care-cloth." Later, a canopy was held over only the bride's head. In Christian weddings, the canopy evolved to the veil, used to hide the bride from the Devil. Up until the mid-1800s, the veil was decorative, hanging down the bride's back, but starting in the second half of the 19th century, it was used to cover her face and conceal her "virgin modesty." These days it's optional.

Bridesmaids

The custom of bridesmaids wearing similar dresses stemmed from primitive marriages in which the intent was to confuse any lurking evil spirits about which woman was the bride. These days the matching dresses seem mainly meant to create a colorful backdrop for the bride's white. ♥

How to Make Your Wedding Stand Out

This is the big day we've all been

waiting for — why not go all out?

With so many people getting married so often, you may find it difficult to plan a wedding that stands apart from the average white-dress affair. Well, don't despair. We've scanned the tabloids, history books, and magazines for clues to what makes a wedding a particularly talked-about event. Following are a few highlights to spark your imagination. Remember, nothing is beyond your supreme bridely being — a palace of princes, a gown that changes into a sexy bathing suit — anything is possible. Be creative. Choose the bridal idea that suits you best, and, who knows, your wedding could end up on a newsstand near you.

Wedding Tip #1
Invite the Whole Country

When 25-year-old Prince Alois, heir to the throne of Liechtenstein, married Duchess Sophie of Bavaria in July of 1993, he made sure his party was bigger than his brother's had been. Not only did the prince invite all 29,000 residents of Liechtenstein, but he rounded up a few big shots, as well: the prince of Monaco, the grand duke of Luxembourg, the crown prince of Spain, and the presidents of Austria and

If it works for royalty, why not for you? A little pomp might make yours a wedding of circumstance.

Switzerland. (The pope couldn't make it; he sent a note.) A few passing tourists weren't sure what all the fuss was about — the concerts and dances and fireworks — but they had a good time anyway.

Wedding Tip #2
Have Your In-laws Pardon Thousands of People on Your Wedding Day

Naruhito's wedding was a liberating experience for thousands.

Although some critics are bound to say that pardoning 30,000 prisoners on your wedding day is opportunistic, you will most certainly

make a good number of friends in the deal. Better yet, declare your wedding day a national holiday — as the parents of Japanese crown prince Naruhito did when he married Masako Owada — and you'll know that the whole country will be happy for you (and for themselves).

Wedding Tip #3
Get Your Father to Spring for an Out-of-the-Ordinary Gift

When Solomon married the pharaoh's daughter, the Egyptian ruler wanted to present his new son-in-law with something nice to mark the occasion. He gave the groom the entire city of Gezer — perhaps the largest wedding present ever.

Wedding Tip #4
Go for the Superlatives

There's nothing like doing things up *big* to gain a spot in the limelight. You'll be a shoe-in for celebrity if you can just top the current record for the most expensive wedding ever. According to Guinness, that would be the nuptials of Mohammed, son of Sheik Rashid Bin Saeed al Maktoum, and Princess Salama, who married in Dubai, United Arab Emirates, in May of 1981. Their wedding, which lasted seven days, was held in a stadium built specifically to hold their 20,000 guests. All told, the wedding tab came to $44 million (give or take a million) — but, what the heck, it was worth every penny.

If you're short on cash but still want to set a record, you can always round up a crowd

The Moon's the limit: a Seoul-ful ceremony.

131

Please Come to Our Wedding; Please Bring Good Gifts

In 1870, the editors of *Godey's Lady's Book* noted that the giving of wedding presents had gotten out of hand, and they recommended that couples send invitations marked "No Presents Received." Despite the magazine's popularity, the advice apparently didn't catch on in the way the editors had intended, for a few years later the magazine had to chastise couples for circulating wedding invitations marked "No Plate Ware."

Heigh yo, silver!

of single friends and try to top the mark for the most people married at one time. The current record stands at 20,825 couples married simultaneously one August day in 1992 by Sun Myung Moon in Seoul, South Korea. (Another 9,800 participated by satellite link.) They did it all at once with a single resounding *ye*.

Wedding Tip #5
Wear a Supersexy Wedding Dress

On her wedding day in June 1986, *Sports Illustrated* swimsuit model Elle Macpherson wore a dress fashioned by Tunisian designer Azzedine Alaia. *People* magazine described her outfit as "a clinging white viscose gown that was a road map to some of the Click model agency's most valuable curves." When things got hot, Macpherson detached a few spare parts and — voilà! — her shoulder and midriff appeared. A little later, she stripped off a few more pieces and flashed a racy bridal bathing suit. It was so revealing, in fact, that when the supermodel saw her mom looking, she blushed.

Wedding Tip #6
Declare Yours the Wedding of the Century

This is a "can't miss" wedding opportunity: Cram 2,500 guests into St. Paul's Cathedral and make sure 700 million viewers in 61 countries tune in to watch on TV. After the ceremony, ride back to the palace in a gilded carriage and instruct the archbishop of Canterbury to grandly proclaim: "Here is the stuff of which fairy tales are made: the prince and princess on their wedding day!"

Although the marriage probably won't last, everyone will remember your absolutely *fabulous* wedding, as they remember Charles and Diana's. And in these circles of fame and fortune that's all that really matters. ♥

Go ahead, Chuck it all, and have a wedding anyone would Di for.

A Cautionary Wedding Tale in Five Parts

We are gathered here today to witness the most embarrassing episode in one couple's life . . .

This is the story of the wedding day from hell. It is a story that is true in all its parts, but not true as a whole, for all these tragedies could not be borne by a single person on a single day. We present this composite picture (taken from the real-life stories of an uncle, a sister, a friend, and master chef Julia Child) as an inspirational tale to show those who dread weddings that their worst fears are bound to be better than what follows. The names, of course, have been changed to protect the (otherwise) blushing brides. Those of weak stomach (or romantic heart) may wish to cover their eyes through the most tragic parts.

I. The Rehearsal

Sue and Bill lived on the West Coast but planned to marry in the East so that Bill's family could attend. They arranged by phone from California for a church on Cape Cod. The minister assured them it would be just what they wanted. Arriving the day before the wedding to rehearse, they found the church defaced by scaffolding on the outside and impassable on the inside. Needless to say, it was not at *all* what they wanted. They fired the minister and scrapped the church.

So it was that on the Saturday before her Sunday wedding — when Sue had yet to arrange for last-minute flowers, get her nails manicured, have her hair done, hem her dress, and meet Bill's relatives for the first time — she was frantically calling around for a place to get married and a minister to perform the ceremony.

With great luck, she managed to find both and still have time to rehearse. The bagpipe player was there and sounded wonderful. The rehearsal went well. Sue felt better. All was ready for the big event — or so they thought.

II. The Night Before the Wedding

That evening Sue and Bill kissed each other good-bye and went their separate ways for the night. Upon arriving at her hotel, Sue was surprised to find a parking lot filled with Mack trucks. She carried her white dress inside, where, to her horror, she found a lobby full of burly truck drivers. They all turned and stared. She tried to slink by unnoticed, but everyone watched her as she passed — the token maiden in the midst of a Mack truck convention. What more could go wrong?

That night she was blasted out of bed by the fire alarm. She panicked about her gown, imagining several months' salary going up in smoke. Clutching her dress to her nightgowned chest, she rushed for the stairs. So did all the truck drivers. It was a scene from *The Poseidon Adventure,* but one, thank heaven, that ended less tragically. It was a false alarm.

Back in bed, she tried to slow her racing heart and get some sleep. It was 1:30. At 2:05 the alarm shook her awake again. She made another dash. At 3:25 it happened again. At 4:00 on the morning of her wedding, Sue finally got to sleep. In her dream, she was climbing from her hotel window down her wedding gown to safety and later arrived at her wedding dressed in a bed sheet.

By morning, the nightmare had ended. Apologizing for the inconvenience, the hotel reimbursed her lodging fee. Sue relaxed, knowing she had used up her share of bad luck. Cetainly nothing else could go wrong.

Or could it?

III. On the Way to the Wedding

En route to her wedding, Sue was struck by the fact that the oncoming truck was headed straight for her car and would actually hit her. It couldn't, she thought; it couldn't. But sure enough, the truck — having lost its brakes — did. Sue was flung onto the side of the road, landing on her head. An ambulance arrived and rushed her to the hospital. There the doctors sewed her scalp together with no fewer than 23 stitches.

Being a good sport, Sue was not deterred from her plans. She arrived at the church wearing a less-than-fashionable bandage. The guests seemed not to mind that she was a little late. In fact, most of the guests had themselves been late, due to the last-minute mix-up of churches and the wrong directions that had been hurriedly given out as a result.

IV. At the Wedding

The bagpipe player was the latest of them all. No one could figure out where he was until someone finally spotted a man in a kilt staggering up the walk. A whiskey flask bulged from his knee sock. The groom rushed out and caught the musician as he stumbled on the steps. The best man gave him coffee; the groom gave him hell. But the bagpipe player wasn't listening; he slumped forward in his chair.

Thirty-five minutes and four cups of coffee later, he tottered to the edge of the balcony to perform the bridal march. The bandaged bride took her place at the foot of the aisle and waited for the music to begin. The bagpipes wheezed and gasped. A screech filled the chapel. Children covered their ears.

Certainly, there is no sound more excruciating to accompany your walk down the aisle on your wedding day than bagpipes played by a drunken man.

Fortunately, the screeching didn't last long. The bagpipe player passed out before the end of the piece, and a heavenly calm settled over the congregation.

V. At the Reception

Having made it through the ceremony looking surprisingly good (despite the bags under her eyes and the bandage on her head), the smiling bride took her place in the receiving line, relieved that the end was in sight.

But wait, what now? The couch-size Mrs. Jones enveloped the size-six bride in an overzealous embrace, and two silk buttons popped off the back of the vintage creamy silk dress, which Sue had had tailored to fit her snugly. The next person in line picked up the buttons and handed them to Sue. A suggestive keyhole had opened on her back, but Sue remained cool. She imagined that her dress had been transformed into a risqué Yves St. Laurent–like fashion. For a moment, the dress continued to hold her braless figure in place, but pressure began to build on the 38 remaining buttons, and soon another button flew free, and another person stooped to pick it up. Everyone was being so nice. By the time they had all made it by her, Sue's hands were full of buttons that they'd handed over.

At the reception, Sue danced with wild abandon past a row of elderly great-aunts. Her tanned back was fully exposed to her waist. They clamped their hands over their mouths. When only one brave button remained, a former boyfriend slipped Sue his tie clasp to keep the final button from breaking free with all the thrill of a champagne cork.

Epilogue: The Morning After

So it is that all bad things must come to an end. Drunken bagpipe players must eventually go on their way (without pay). And wedding videotapes can be doctored. A labored edit of the whole horrid affair can transform bagpipe screeching into the remarkably calming strains of Pachelbel's Canon. And a West Coast reception, held weeks after the East Coast ceremony, offers enough distance and daring to make the couple swear that, yes, just as you see here on the video, our wedding was truly a flawless affair. And, yes, of course, it can only mean that they will live happily ever after (at least in their home video version). ♥

Never Gamble with the Gods of Superstition

Especially on the day when you've got everything to lose.

By now you've realized that the odds against even the best-planned wedding going off without some sort of disaster are slim. And yet you have invested an outrageous sum of money, an agonizing year of planning, and a disproportionate degree of emotion in the preparation. Given all that, you are ready to try almost anything (short of elopement) to escape the mounting dread.

Only one possibility remains: throw your fate to the gods of superstition. Your friends may think you a fool, but you've got nothing to lose and maybe everything to gain. Folk beliefs, after all, have been followed faithfully since the day before forever, so there must be something to them (if only tradition). As the author of *The Folklore of Weddings and Marriage* writes, "It would be utter folly — on the day — to throw all tradition out the window. You can wager the new dime in the heel of your left shoe that your grandmother didn't, and your daughter won't!" Who knows, superstitions may save the day — and even your marriage.

We've got a creeping suspicion that this little fellow will bring the bride luck.

Good Luck Omens You Can Control

☛ Enter and leave the church on your right foot for luck and happiness in the years to come. (All will be lost, however, should you fall flat on your face.)

☛ Wear gold earrings on your wedding day to achieve eternal bliss.

☛ Feed a cat out of your wedding shoe for good luck.

☛ Marry in June, named for Juno, the goddess of marriage, who offers prosperity to the man and happiness to the woman who wed during her month. Avoid May if you can, for May is the month of unhappy death.

☞ Wear something old from a happily married woman, something borrowed for good fortune, something blue for heavenly true love, and a dime in the left shoe for riches.

☞ Sew a penny into the seam of your wedding dress for luck on your wedding day and in later years.

Good Luck Omens You Can't Control (But Can Hope For)

☞ A spider crawling on the bride's gown during the ceremony symbolizes good luck.

☞ Fortune will come to the bride whose veil is ripped at the altar. (So will the repair bills.)

☞ If a ray of sun shines on the bride's head as she leaves the church, domestic bliss will follow.

Just Plain Bad Luck

☞ If you're the bride, don't rehearse the ceremony on the day before the wedding, or even read the marriage service; either of these actions will bring bad luck.

☞ Don't let the groom see your wedding dress before the ceremony begins, or you will doom your luck.

☞ If you part with a wedding gift, you will part with happiness.

☞ Don't make your own gown, tear it, or spill wine on it; all bode bad fortune.

☞ Because pearls are the symbols of tears, it is said that for each pearl the bride wears on her wedding day, her husband will give her that many reasons for crying.

Tying the Knot

In the days of the Romans, brides wore wedding girdles, which were fastened with knots for the grooms to undo. The expression "to tie the knot" dates back to that time, but it's been common since then in wedding ceremonies around the world. In India, a marriage was once considered legal and binding when the Hindu groom had secured a ribbon around the throat of his bride. And in ancient Carthage, a bride and groom got hitched by having their thumbs joined with a leather strip.

My Wife, the Log

Among the Brahmins of southern India, custom once demanded that an older brother marry before a younger brother did. If the older brother hadn't found a bride by the time his junior was ready to marry, however, there was a way around the custom. The older brother could marry a tree. This left the younger one free to take a wife — with the custom intact. At other times, a tree wedding was held during a regular wedding so that any evil spirits present would land and dwell not with the bridal couple but with the tree.

☛ When getting dressed for your wedding, do not eat anything if you want to avoid bad luck (and indigestion).

☛ Never whistle near the wedding dress; this lures sinister spirits.

☛ Be careful around the wedding gifts. It is said that if, on her wedding day, the bride should break an item, she and her mother-in-law will argue, and the new husband will align with his mother.

☛ A gown hemmed with black thread brings death (and looks terrible).

☛ Never put on your veil before your wedding day. If you do, you may be deserted, have an unhappy marriage, or even die before the wedding. (Seems a little drastic, we know, but the gods of superstition are a tempestuous bunch.)

Who Will Wear the Britches — The Bride or the Groom?

☛ The bride who stands at the altar with her right foot in front of the groom's will ensure future influence over her husband-to-be.

☛ The groom who spots the bride before she sees him will rule during marriage.

☛ Whoever's thumb is on top when the couple takes hands at the altar will head the household.

☛ After the wedding, whoever drinks a glass of water first will be the one in charge. ♥

Going to the Civil Service of Love

The Puritans considered a wedding to be more of a civil occasion than a sacrosanct one, so they forbade ministers to perform the ceremony. Eventually, clergymen did gain legal permission to officiate at weddings, but in most cases the colonial couples continued to choose a magistrate or justice of the peace over a minister. Not until the early 1800s did the number of civil marriages decline. And not until the end of the 19th century did the church weddings we take for granted become common practice for middle-class Americans.

141

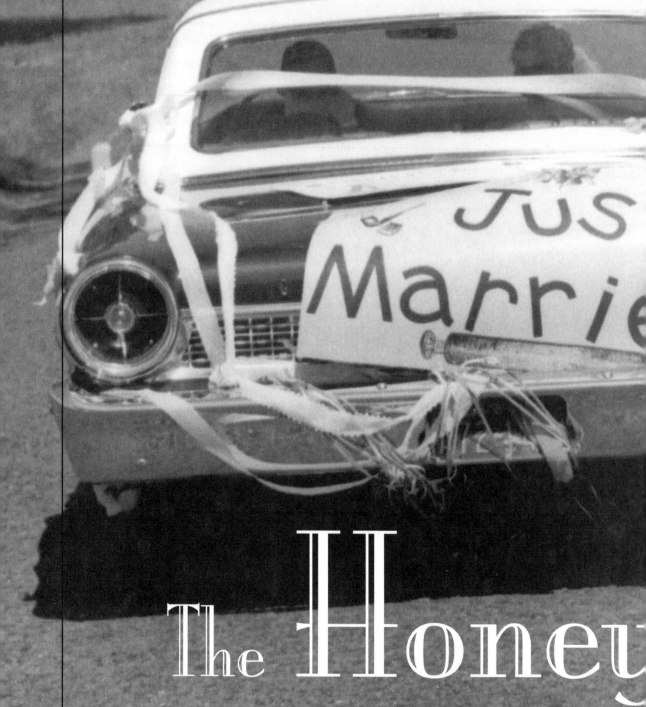

II

The Honey

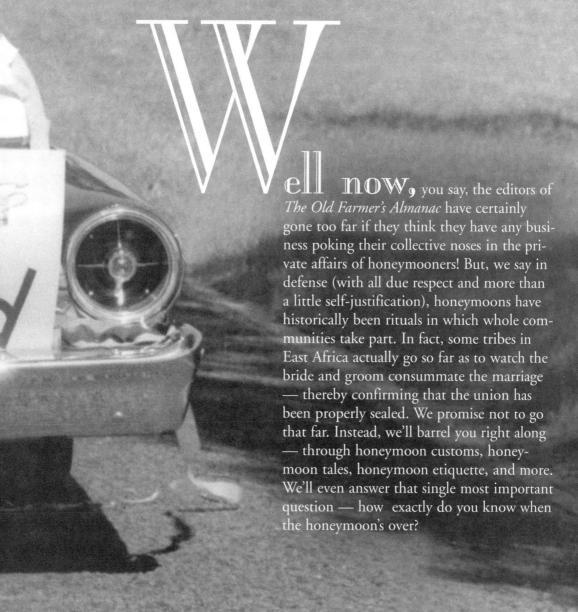

Well now,

you say, the editors of *The Old Farmer's Almanac* have certainly gone too far if they think they have any business poking their collective noses in the private affairs of honeymooners! But, we say in defense (with all due respect and more than a little self-justification), honeymoons have historically been rituals in which whole communities take part. In fact, some tribes in East Africa actually go so far as to watch the bride and groom consummate the marriage — thereby confirming that the union has been properly sealed. We promise not to go that far. Instead, we'll barrel you right along — through honeymoon customs, honeymoon tales, honeymoon etiquette, and more. We'll even answer that single most important question — how exactly do you know when the honeymoon's over?

moon

How to Say "I Abducted Your Daughter" in Norwegian

The peculiar evolution of that ancient custom we call the honeymoon.

The greatest handicap with which to start a marriage seems to me to be the well-entrenched custom of the Honeymoon. . . . Someone, years ago, thought up the idea and it has stayed with us ever since, unsettling nine marriages out of ten before they even get started . . . and though they have the one advantage of being a trip (marriage provides very few of these in later days), even that is countered by too many disadvantages.
— Bell Wiley, *So You're Going to Get Married*

Let's just be blunt about it: what Bell Wiley wrote back in 1938 still remains a secret gripe of many brides today. Your honeymoon just didn't match the

Attila the Honeymoon: A lesson in moderation from an unlikely source.

promised bliss that everyone else seems to have enjoyed. Perhaps you were so exhausted from the wedding preparations and execution that you, as Ms. Wiley puts it so nicely, simply could not make the physical response you thought automatic. Although all you *really* longed for was 24 hours of undisturbed sleep, you had to keep up the charade of romantic euphoria. Perhaps you came face to face with the disappointing realization that the two of you have almost nothing in common. After a yearlong buildup to three days of wedding hubbub, you suddenly realize that you are now hitched for eternity (and eternity is looking like a long time) to a guy who has taken to snoring or belching or *whatever*. Perhaps you are wondering if you're the only one who has ever had these less-than-ecstatic thoughts on your honeymoon (or shortly thereafter).

If Only They Had Told You . . .

Well, no. The historic fact of the matter is that the honeymoon from its start has had shady associations. It originated in ancient Scandinavia as a form of abduction (hardly a nice thing at all). The custom was for a man to steal a maiden from a neighboring village (or wherever he could find her) and take her into seclusion. The Norse language referred to this as *hjunotts-manathr*. After a month in hiding, the kidnapped bride would most likely have become pregnant, and the situation irreversible.

To the French it was a *lune de miel,* or literally a "moon of honey." Northern Europeans understood the "honeymoon" to be bittersweet, because it was only one month out of many and the following moon cycles would never be able to match the first. British poets of the 16th and 17th centuries often used the word *honeymooning* to represent an expected waxing and waning of affection between partners. Likewise, folk belief held that after the honeymoon achieved its full passion, it would invariably turn lukewarm, so that the cooling passion could make room for a more settled relationship.

Others attribute the etymology of *honeymoon* to the practice of newlyweds in parts of ancient Europe who drank a daily cup of honeyed wine (called *metheglin,* or mead) for 30 days after the wedding. Attila the Hun drank plenty of mead at his wedding feast in 450 A.D., and even more at another feast a few years later — after which he vomited, went into a stupor, and died of overindulgence. (Whether you're the groom — or bride — or a guest, take heed.)

Excessive pleasure comes at a great cost. You are allowed to indulge your affections, but only to a degree. Sometimes

The Honeymoon That (Almost) Wasn't

In January 1987, Janet Ciampanelli, a first-grade teacher from North Providence, Rhode Island, met a gray-black kitten named Ernie at the Coventry Animal Hospital where she volunteered. The kitten had been burned and abandoned and would need $5,000 worth of plastic surgery. Janet had that much money in her Hawaii honeymoon fund. Without a second thought, she decided to sacrifice it for the cat. During the seven weeks it took Ernie to recover in the incubator, Janet fed him cat food from her fingertip. By June, Ernie was well enough to take part in Janet and Louis D'Agostino's wedding. He (the cat, that is) wore bandages and a dashing bow.

When word got out in the newspaper that Janet and Louis had sacrificed their honeymoon to save a sorry kitten, people were touched. They sent $7,000 worth of donations. Janet spent it on a second skin graft for Ernie and on a fund to help mistreated animals. Great for the animals, not so great for the man.

But the story didn't end there. A couple who had read about Ernie and who ran a bed-and-breakfast in Bucksport, Maine, wrote to say that they'd put Louis and Janet up in a honeymoon suite overlooking the ocean for as long as they'd like — for free. Janet and Louis wouldn't have gone if Ernie couldn't go, too. But he could. And they did. And so their honeymoon happened after all, and happened happily at that.

147

American Falls from Goat Island, Niagara Falls N. Y.

"Dear Folks, Having a great time. Glad you're not here."

it will seem that others have more say than you do in how much you can carry on with your new spouse. Indeed, the world will watch with folded arms. "Newlyweds should try not to overdo their togetherness, as it can be embarrassing to other people in social situations," instructs the author of *Amy Vanderbilt's Complete Book of Etiquette.* "They should not expect to be seated next to each other at dinner parties. As a married couple, they will find that they are supposed to spread their charm elsewhere at the dinner table, not solely to each other!"

What's more, the first thing a couple must do upon arriving at their honeymoon spot is to call both sets of parents. "Everyone at home will be exhausted and in a state of sentimental euphoria after your wedding," Vanderbilt writes, and will be anxiously awaiting a thank-you. The well-prepared honeymooners will have tucked away a long list of all those requiring acknowledgment of their gifts and will diligently proceed to spend their honeymoon phoning or writing each one on the list. "A thank-you note for a wedding present written during a wedding trip," Vanderbilt contends, "is the nicest thank you of all."

The fact that we must worry about such public courtesies at a time of intimate seclusion stems in part from the 19th-century evolution of the honeymoon. In the early 1800s, honeymoons — or "wedding trips," as they were called then — were meant to establish a relationship not between the partners themselves, but between the community and the couple. At that time, newlyweds spent their post-wedding weeks at the homes of family and friends. If, for some reason, the new husband and wife did return right away to their own home, a band of neighbors and visitors would follow to keep them company for weeks on end.

Wedding Trips Take a U-Turn

By the 1830s, transportation had improved enough to allow for cheaper, quicker, more far-ranging travel. Men were less frequently tied to daily farm jobs and more likely to be able to take time off from the store or office for a bridal trip. More couples, therefore, began to spend their "nuptial journeys" visiting popular sites such as Niagara Falls, Vermont's Green Mountains, and New York City.

Within a decade, the norm was for couples to arrange their honeymoon trips as much around place as around people, but even then it was common for friends and relatives to come along for the ride. Traveling companions helped keep the couple connected to the community and eased the transition from the fun of courtship to the responsibilities and exclusivity of married life.

In later years, as American society became even more mobile and American communities became less central in newly married couples' lives, honeymoons became more far-ranging and intimate affairs. Couples opted to spend their honeymoon alone together forming a stronger bond between them and apart from their friends and families. (In a similar vein, the Bulgarians long ago sent newlyweds off for a week, sequestering them for a time during which no one could go into — or come out of — the newlyweds' den.)

During the early part of this century, the typical wedding trip often lasted three to four weeks, and those in wealthy circles would take four to six *months* to make their way around the world on a leisurely ocean liner. Nowadays, people are more practical (or poorer, or more tied to busy lives and work schedules) and generally tend to keep their honeymoons short. Of those polled for a recent Harlequin Romance Report, 52 percent said that a one-week honeymoon would be enough. Only

5 percent said that they'd like to go
for a month or more. A full 33 percent said that a weekend (*a measly two
days!*) would do, and 10 percent opted
for only two weeks.

For that brief time, the places couples choose are what you'd expect.
The top three honeymoon destina-
tions, according to that same Harlequin report, are the Caribbean, Italy,
and Hawaii (with the runners-up
being the Canadian Rockies, California, France, and upstate New York).
Only a few folks make choices like that
of the Miami couple who, in 1959,
holed up for fun in a bomb shelter.

Wherever the destination, the
honeymoon is supposed to be, as
*Merriam Webster's Collegiate Dictio-
nary* says, "a period of unusual harmony esp. following the establishment
of a new relationship." And certainly
enough couples must have found
some harmony on their trips together
to have kept the tradition alive all
these years. In fact, a whole industry
has grown up to cater to their desires: tourist bureaus package trips
for them; developers build hotels;
publishers put out fat books of des-
tinations. Each year people go back
again and again for a second honeymoon, a third, a fourth, a tenth
— so that it seems, in the end, no
matter what the drawbacks they encounter, couples are still having a
grand time trying like crazy to get
their honeymoons happy enough
to spill a little bliss into the years of
marriage that follow. ♥

"Newlyweds should try not to overdo their togetherness," Amy Vanderbilt advised, "as it can be embarrassing to other people in social situations."

151

"A Funny Thing Happened on My Honeymoon"

Three Almanac readers reveal private moments from the most private of times.

I. A Candid Camera Moment

It was 1956, and we were honeymooning in Miami.

"Are you coming to the beach, dear?" my wife of 24 hours asked from the bathroom, where she was changing into her bathing suit.

"I'll join you later," I said. "I want to get a picture of the skyline from the roof of the hotel."

"I'll wave to you," she said. "Take my picture."

"OK," I replied, naive enough to think that a camera I'd bought for $9.95, including two rolls of film, could take a picture from 15 stories high.

It was a short flight of stairs to the roof, and I was so involved in adjusting the various settings on the camera that I failed to see the sign on the door that led to the roof. I heard screaming before I saw the eight naked sunbathing women. Terrified of what my bride would think, I turned to flee, only to discover that on my side of the door there was no handle. I turned, saw an exit sign, dropped the camera, and ran.

In the lobby that evening, there was a note on the bulletin board explaining where one could claim a lost camera. It's probably still there.

— *William Polsky, Montreal, Quebec*

II. Just Married — Just Ask Mom

Full of desire, we checked into a motel to spend our wedding night in the summer of 1953. Never having registered as "married," my husband innocently signed his name and my maiden name, and we went to our room. We were sipping champagne when a knock rattled the door. Opening it, we found the disgruntled motel owner.

"I don't allow singles to stay together!" he roared, reminding us of our names in his book.

We assured him that it was a mistake and we were married. But since I had no identification, he told us to leave.

"Let us telephone our parents, and they'll tell you that we're married," my husband pleaded. The owner agreed, but only if we went back to the motel lobby.

No answer at my mom's house. "I'll try again," I sobbed. Again meant four more times, and the owner's suspicious look made us feel very "unmarried."

"One more try," he sneered.

At 1:15 A.M., Mom answered her phone. She'd been out celebrating with our wedding guests. With reddened face, the owner sheepishly grinned when Mom confirmed our marriage.

Exhausted and back in our room — ready to show our love for each other — we fell asleep!

— *Jean Powis, Troy, New York*

III. The Perfect Honeymoon Breakfast

My husband and I were married in Albuquerque, New Mexico, on April 20, 1951. After our ceremony, we left in my father's pickup truck for our honeymoon "western style." I was from the East and in awe of the beautiful southwestern landscapes and of my handsome young husband.

We camped in the desert, our "honeymoon suite" being the back of the pickup truck. The next morning we realized we had forgotten our grub box and all we had to eat were four raw potatoes. My husband fired up an old Coleman stove and fried the potatoes for our honeymoon breakfast. Then he walked into the desert and picked me a large, beautiful red cactus bloom.

Later we drove to the nearest small town and bought ice cream at a roadside stand.

Forty years later, we still laugh about our "honeymoon breakfast" of fried potatoes and ice cream.

— *Mrs. James S. Lunsford, Los Alamos, New Mexico* ♥

12 Sure-fire Ways to Get Off to a Good Start

We wouldn't, after all, want you to go into

your honeymoon unprepared.

In case your mother never told you what to expect, we offer forthwith a dozen tips to help you get the most out of that superspecial night and all the golden days that follow.

Four Suggestions to Do with the Bridal Chamber

1. To guard against evil that a spurned lover may wish on the newly married couple, fumigate the closed bedchamber with burning leaves and bramble fruit.

2. The herbs sacred to Venus (marjoram, meadowsweet, mint, thyme, and violet) are said to be love-inducing when mixed with those herbs sacred to Mars (basil and broom). Spread them on the floor, or scent the bridal sheets with them to evoke feelings of love.

3. A verbena sprig, said to release an aphrodisiac scent, is just the thing to sneak inside the pillowcases of the bridal chamber.

4. The long, thin shape of the mandrake root is believed to stimulate sexual longing, so hang one at the head of the honeymoon bed and see what happens. (Take care, though, not to eat the powdered root,

The Sounds of Silence

The Latins were the first to serenade newly married couples. They called the practice *shivaree*. The ancient provinces of France also enjoyed the custom, but they called it *charivari*. The latter version relied less on romantic music and more on boisterous noise banged out on the backs of tin pans and kettles. The French people of Canada and Louisiana introduced the loud horseplay to American honeymooners. And wedding couples (thank heaven) learned that they could earn relief from the rowdy serenade by showering silver coins upon the merrymakers.

The Honeymooners

When *The Honeymooners* television show first broke off from the *Cavalcade of Stars* in 1955, the original title of the new sitcom was to be *The Beast*. It would have fit the intended characters: a shrew of a wife named Alice Kramden, who put her big-mouthed husband, Ralph Kramden, in his place. But Jackie Gleason, who produced the show and created much of his own dialogue, stepped in to make the husband a more sympathetic character and to suggest that an underlying love be played out between the couple. Because of that, the name *The Beast* didn't fit, but *The Honeymooners* did. The show became such a hit that a fan club called RALPH (Royal Association for the Longevity and Preservation of the Honeymooners) was formed. Fans memorized every word of all 39 original shows. (Imagine if couples devoted as much effort to their own marriages!)

If Only He'd Been Researching Aphrodisiacs . . .

Although you may think it productive in the short term to combine work and pleasure on your honeymoon, it will inevitably make your spouse grumpy in the long term. A good case in point is the Massachusetts rose grower who spent his honeymoon driving to Chicago (and back) so that he could stop at every greenhouse along the way while his wife sat in the car. Unfortunately, he was not searching out the most beautiful rose for his new bride. He was, in fact, doing business. And although he did become the second-largest grower in the state, he didn't ingratiate himself with his new wife. She was heard to complain on many occasions that the only roses he brought home were the old ones that needed studying for flaws. A very thorny situation to be sure.

or its narcotic properties will bring on sleepiness — or even death, which won't do any good at all).

Two to Do with Dressing

5. When the bride removes her wedding attire, she should throw a stocking over her left shoulder. Beyond exciting the eager groom, this custom is believed to determine the bride's future luck. If the stocking falls in a straight line on the floor, her luck will be ongoing. If not, it will be uneven. (A good dose of starch might help matters here.)

6. Tradition says a woman must discard every pin from her wedding apparel. If even a single pin is kept, everything will go wrong for the new bride — and who needs that sort of bad luck when married life is challenging enough as it is? (Likewise, if a bridesmaid keeps a pin, a year will pass before she weds.)

There's something to be said for sweeping a girl off her feet.

Let's Not Get Carried Away

Some say the custom of carrying the bride over the threshold took root among the ancient Romans. The Romans believed that evil spirits gathered in doorways and that a bride who stumbled during her vulnerable transition time would forever be unlucky in marriage.

Others believe that the custom of sweeping the bride off her feet originated with the actual abduction, or carrying off, of the bride in ancient times. It was customary then for the bride to kick and scream when she was taken from her family's house and carried by the groom over the threshold of her new home.

These days most brides would consider it simply a romantic gesture (while most fellows would consider it a little hard on the back).

158

Four to Do with Sleeping

7. On the first night of your honeymoon, do not sleep in your new house. Custom says that if you do, bad luck will linger like mildew around a leaking toilet bowl.

8. Wherever you end up sleeping on your wedding night, make sure your heads face north, so that you and your spouse will follow the compass point of happiness throughout your married life.

9. The bride must have a pair of slippers or socks handy on her wedding night so that her bare feet do not touch the floor and tickle her with misfortune (not to mention giving her cold feet).

10. It is said (though we hate to tell you this) that the one who falls asleep first on the wedding night will be the first to die. That may seem grim news to the exhausted bride and groom, until they realize it is a good incentive to stay awake till dawn, reveling in carnal bliss.

A Final Two to Do with Evil Spirits

11. Whatever you do, *don't* let an ex-lover who carries hatred in his heart kiss you, the bride (or the groom, for that matter), on your wedding day; otherwise you will have a horrible honeymoon ahead.

12. Folklore says that a broom and bowl of salt placed in the entryway of the honeymoon bedchamber will guard the newlyweds from witches. The witch, you see, must stop to count each straw on the broom and each grain of salt in the bowl before she can pass inside. By the time she has finished the task, dawn will surely have broken and the couple will be safe. Thank goodness. ♥

Be Sure to Pack a Little Common Sense

If you're getting married for the second (or third or fourth) time, do not return to the honeymoon spot where you took your first (or second or third) spouse — no matter how much fun you had there. What's more, do not take your kids by a previous marriage on your honeymoon. A six-year-old splashing water on the floor from the Jacuzzi is sure to dampen the romantic mood.

How Do You Know When the Honeymoon's Over?

Four real-life disaster stories make the answer all too clear.

I. A Long Drive Home

These days Dolly Parton does things up big, but when she married Carl Dean back in May 1966, things were much simpler; she had only one day to get married and have a honeymoon. Wanting to keep the news of her wedding out of the Nashville newspapers, Dolly drove with Carl and her mother to Ringold, Georgia. On the way, they stopped at Sears to purchase a simple pair of rings (using Carl's mother's credit card to pay for them and working many years to clear the debt later).

For the ceremony at the First Baptist Church, Carl wore a dark suit and Dolly a short white dress and veil. When it was over, there was, as Dolly would later say, "no party, no champagne, no cake." There was only the long drive back to Nashville . . . and the sinking realization, when they had gotten a good part of the way home, that Dolly's mother had left her purse back at the church.

The drive to retrieve it took up most of the couple's half-day honeymoon. The next day they were back at work.

From The Old Farmer's Almanac

He who consults his spouse will have a good counselor. I have heard our minister say, "Woman's instincts are often truer than man's reason." They jump at a thing at once and are wise offhand. Say what you will of your wife's advice, it's likely you'll be sorry you did not take it.

—1889

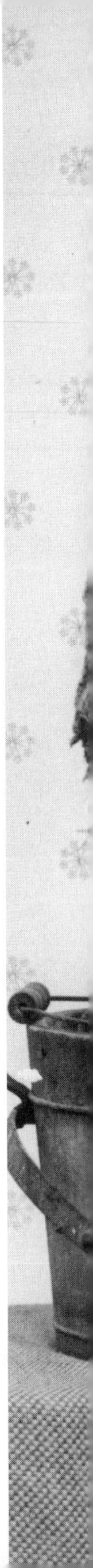

II. A Short Drive Home

In 1878, John and Frances lived on neighboring farms. They met in church, as most young people did in the Victorian era, and John proceeded to woo the petite, brown-haired beauty with the heart-shaped face. Before long, he asked her father's consent to marry her.

The wedding took place in a log church, and the congregation

was proud of their first Lutheran wedding in the wilderness. It was a wonderful excuse for every member of the congregation to don his or her church clothes, curry the horses, dust off the buggy, and have a fine day of meeting and greeting and putting their stamp of approval on that way of life.

After the reception, John and Fannie (as she was familiarly known by the late afternoon of their wedding day) climbed into his buggy to ride to his farmhouse. On the way, they saw, off in the distance, the approaching wagon of a man about whom John said to Fannie, "Do not raise your eyes as we pass — I have no use for that man."

As their respective vehicles passed in the narrow road, Fannie noted that the man was an old family friend, and she raised her eyes and spoke a warm greeting. John drove past his farmhouse to her home and deposited Fannie there with her parents and family.

Fannie, with the help of her father, obtained a divorce from John on the grounds that the marriage had not been consummated.

— *Courtesy of Ruth J. Newcomer, Hillard, Ohio*

III. The Honeymoon Suite That Wasn't

My husband and I stayed in the Hostería la Cienega in Cotopaxi, Ecuador. Upon checking out, my husband questioned the room rate.

The clerk explained that we had been in the honeymoon suite — the only room with a double bed.

After some discussion back and forth about the charge, my husband's point, "But I am a seventy-one-year-old man; I could not take full advantage of the honeymoon suite," was met with amusement and a reduction — and later with a complaint from me that the romance must be truly gone from our marriage when we spend the night in the honeymoon suite and my husband asks for a refund!

— *Courtesy of Sally Reeds, Beaufort, South Carolina*

IV. Head Over Heels in Love (& Out of Luck)

Even the best-planned honeymoons can come to less-than-romantic ends. Take, for instance, the story of Jamie Kageleiry and Craig Mac-Cormack, who, having successfully made it through the wedding ceremony and reception, were ready to relax on their honeymoon in tranquil Bermuda.

On their second day there, they went off together to tour the island in tandem on a rented moped. Craig steered, and Jamie wrapped her arms around him. Both were happy. The island was beautiful. There was so much to see. There in the field beyond a stone wall stood some cows. Jamie spotted them first. How strange, she thought, to see cows in Bermuda. "Moooo," she shouted into Craig's ear, and pointed at the cows.

Later, people would tell them you're not *both* supposed to turn your heads suddenly while riding tandem on a moped. But Jamie and Craig didn't know that then — when they crashed into the stone wall.

Craig was fine. Jamie was not. That night, after leaving the hospital in a hip cast, Jamie would need both Craig *and* a cabdriver to carry her over the threshold.

"I wanted to make you see stars on our honeymoon," Craig said, "but not like that."

For the next nine months, Jamie couldn't walk much. She had lived with Craig for three years before they married; now, a week after their abbreviated honeymoon, she was forced to move from their fifth-floor walkup back home to be cared for by her parents.

Jamie's father had a talk with Craig. "Listen," he said, "I told you to *carry* her over the threshold, not *throw* her over it."

There was nothing more to say. The honeymoon was over. ♥

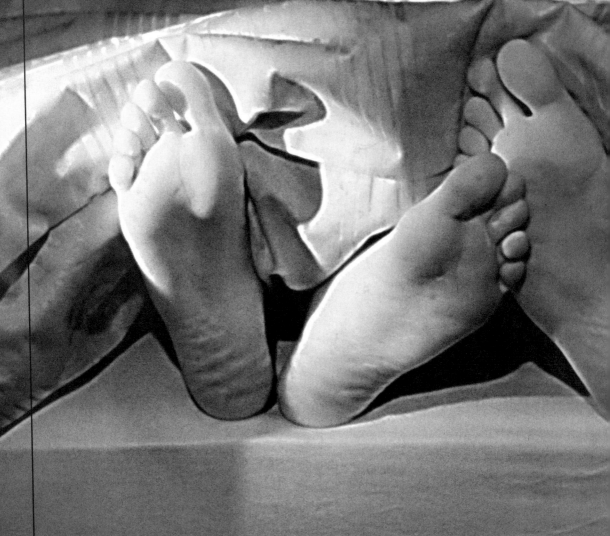

Sex

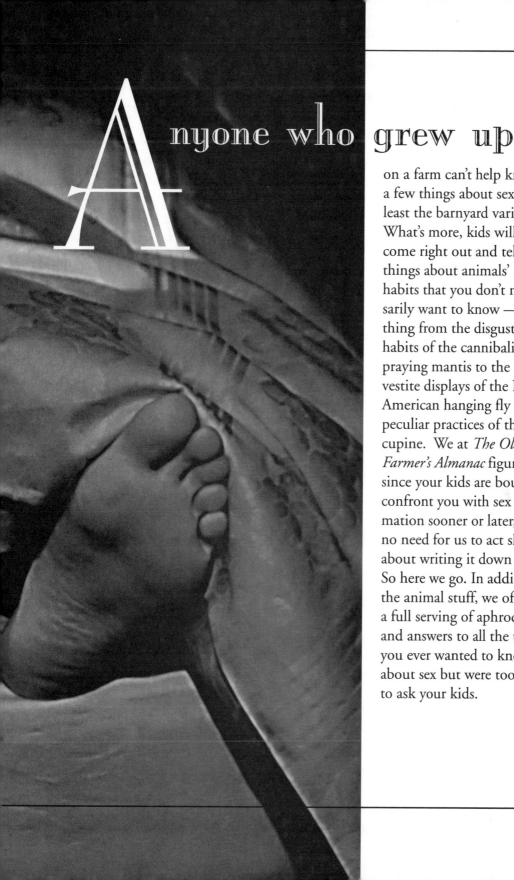

Anyone who grew up

on a farm can't help knowing a few things about sex — at least the barnyard variety. What's more, kids will often come right out and tell you things about animals' mating habits that you don't necessarily want to know — everything from the disgusting habits of the cannibalistic praying mantis to the transvestite displays of the North American hanging fly to the peculiar practices of the porcupine. We at *The Old Farmer's Almanac* figure that since your kids are bound to confront you with sex information sooner or later, there's no need for us to act shy about writing it down now. So here we go. In addition to the animal stuff, we offer you a full serving of aphrodisiacs and answers to all the things you ever wanted to know about sex but were too afraid to ask your kids.

Peculiar Mating Habits in the Animal Kingdom

Passion, cannibalism, gender switching, and more — all are represented in the the lurid world of animal sex.

All the world is queer,
Saving thee and me,
And even thee is a little queer.
— Unknown

The praying mantis does it with consuming passion.

Well, someone should say it if the scientists won't: animal sex is downright odd. Anyone who knows anything about the bizarre and kinky habits of the natural world will agree. Consider the evidence at hand (adult discretion advised).

You have probably heard that the female praying mantis will bite the head off the male while they are mating. *(How rude of her!)* But have you heard that the lower half of the male will continue to copulate even after its top half has been consumed? *(How thoughtless of him!)* And what should we make of the barbaric female sea worm, who abruptly turns on an unsuspecting male and munches the tail — testes and all — right off? *(Ouch!)* Then, leaving the poor guy spermless, she wriggles off to digest her sadistic snack and wait for the sperm to fertilize her eggs. *(Just imagine the*

Like James Dean, the snail is really a softie underneath.

country-and-western song that guy could write!)

Leeches at least have affirmative action abuse. Half the time he gets it, half the time she does — or so it seems. As hermaphrodites, they have the peculiar habit of switching sexes. On mating day, whoever chooses to be the male grabs hold of a nearby female and plunks a flesh-chewing sac of sperm on her skin. (No, a four-year-old *did not* make this up.) When the enzyme has torn a hole in her skin, the sperm go to work on her eggs, and before you know it there are many more hideous leechettes trying hard to suck blood from between your toes.

One more cannibalistic creature, just to make the point before we move on. The name of the black widow spider suggests death, but who'd have thought that she'd cold-bloodedly devour up to *25 mates* in one day? Don't those guys ever learn?

Casanovas of the Wild

Not all in the animal kingdom is so unpleasant. Let us turn to the most romantic of specimens — that slimy creature who hides out in a seemingly impermeable shell: the snail. The snail is the James Dean of the animal kingdom — a male with a tough, remote demeanor that disguises a soft center. Only once in his life will the snail emerge to cuddle with a female. But when he does, he'll wallow in it. He'll hold tight to his love for up to *12 hours* with what naturalist David Quammen poetically describes as a "sinuous, groping tube . . . that's ex-

Dumb Love

Evolutionary psychology has shown a difference in how men and women choose sex partners. In one survey, men and women were asked, "What would be the lowest level of intelligence you would accept in a person you were dating?" Both said, in general, that they would accept an average level of intelligence. They were next asked how low a level of intelligence they would accept from someone they were going to have sex with. The women said that their date would have to have a much higher level of intelligence. The men said that a much lower level of intelligence would do.

Yow! For porcupines, diplomacy is paramount.

☞ **From The** ☜
Old Farmer's Almanac

Having migrated to the mating pools in early spring, the male toads put their vocal equipment to work in the breeding chorus, whose sound may carry as much as a half mile or more.... So strong is the mating drive that some males have even been discovered grasping attractive lumps of mud along the shorelines.

— 1994

truded, at will, like an idea from the snail's head." *(O slimy joy!)*

And what of porcupines, you ask — how *do* they do it? What about those quills? If you were a porcupine, you'd find a way, and here's what you'd do. If you were a male, you'd make yourself attractive to a female, luring her out of a tree with low vocal grunts. Then you'd shower her with spurts of urine, chase her around, wrestle her, and shower her with more urine — grunting all the while. (We *told* you this would get kinky.) The female would finally succumb, and things would be as they must for the perpetuation of the species. In other words, the female would assume the position: raise her hindquarters and stretch her tail over her back to provide a convenient quill-free staging. The male would rest his quill-free chest on the platform with his forelegs dangling. He'd do his business quickly and forcefully to ensure proper insemination, then he'd take a break and clean up a bit. When he'd caught his breath, he'd continue copulating as before. The two would repeat the act as often as desired until one or the other climbed a tree and screamed and lunged angrily at the partner. At that point, the interlude would officially end.

Yes, the males of many species are talented creatures and will go to great lengths to impress the females. That includes the most romantic of rodents, the lesser mole rat, who painstakingly constructs not only an elaborate subterranean house of halls and storerooms, bedrooms and bathrooms (sealed off when full), but also a special "wedding chamber" exclusively reserved for mating.

The love nest built by the male knot-tying weaverbird must be female-approved or she won't do the deed. What's worse, if he does a shoddy job of construction, she'll make him take the whole thing apart and start from scratch. *(Nag, nag, nag!)*

On the kinder end of the spectrum, there's the female red-eyed tree frog, who carries her mate around on her back, then lifts him over the threshold and sets him gently down to fertilize her eggs. (Chivalry in reverse.)

When the Sexes Swap Places

And then there are those devious females who aren't really females at all, but male red-sided garter snakes in drag. What a "she-male" does, according to two observant University of Texas scientists, is lure up

The male red-sided garter snake has to be alluring to males *and* females — what a drag!

The Safe Sex Sofa

Safe sex is all the rage these days, but not necessarily all the fun free sex used to be. A recent advance, however, may help us lighten up on the matter. It's called the Safe Sex Sofa, and its two pieces sell for $6,000. When you sit on either its flower-shaped chair or its long chaise, the sofa plays messages that encourage you to have responsible sex. If nothing else, it makes for (literally) a good conversation piece.

to 100 males to him. Then he slips off from the pack and gets the real female to himself. It's a good trick: in 29 out of 42 tests, the impostor got to the female first and had his way with her.

The trick works, too, for the stickleback fish. By mimicking a female fish, the sneaker gains entrance into another male's harem. Once inside, he spreads his sperm where the other guy formerly had exclusive rights.

But the sneakiest transvestite of all is the North American hanging fly, who tricks another male suitor into giving up his sex lure (a delicious dead insect), then uses the bait to attract his own female sex partner. "This not only puts the other male at a disadvantage," writes Mark Jerome Walters in *Courtship in the Animal Kingdom,* "but saves the mimicker from the risky task of capturing a gift, during which time he must expose himself to the ever present danger of spider webs."

So you see that sex can be a nasty, backstabbing business. But animal sex is not all bad news. The male bowerbird is a romantic lover. He devotes his time and energy to gathering flowers, feathers, berries, colored paper, and glass to decorate the love bower he builds for his mate. Nothing is too much for him if it means winning the interest of a female. Even after he has won her and they have mated, he will set to work again to build a sturdier nest for their young. The bower remains standing but goes unused in the future; it's simply a testament of his devotion.

Woo her with flowers, or anything else to decorate the honeymoon nest. It's a sure bet for the bowerbird.

Last — and perhaps best — are the monkeys who have been called the sexiest of primates: the bonobos. Whenever they get the chance, they'll fool around with anyone and everyone in the tribe. Sexual contact is their way not only of showing affection but also of avoiding fights. Sex, in other words, is the bonobo's version of the motto "Make love not war" — which for monkeys (or men) is not a bad idea at that. ♥

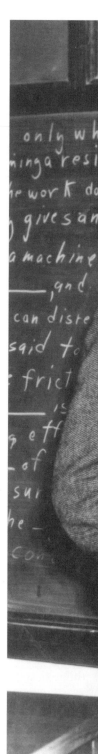

How to Teach Your Parents About the Birds & the Bees

There are a few things they really ought to know, and chances are they won't ask. So it's up to you to sit them down and have that little talk.

> *It is of the utmost importance, in imparting sex knowledge to one's parents, that it be done in such a way as not to engender fear or anxiety. The phraseology should be chosen carefully, and efforts should be made to explain everything clearly but without the use of words which have a tendency to make old people nervous. The word "erotic" is such a word.*
> — James Thurber and E. B. White, *Is Sex Necessary?*

Nothing is more essential to the perpetuation of the species, yet nothing has been more misunderstood. Cloudy analogies linking sex to birds and bees, to storks and swamp mud, have done little to clarify matters. In fact, after all these years, it is very likely that nobody *really* knows what they are talking about. When it comes to the specifics of making babies, it is all just a big mystery. Granted, there have been a number of theories put forth on the matter, and each

Really — it's simple.

Old MacDonald had a farm — and nobody had to teach sex ed to *his* kid . . .

has its own merits, but there's still a need to get the information more widely understood. The time has come to have that little talk. And, of course, the traditional way to begin is with . . .

What the Barnyard Animals Know

Historically, people have learned about sex by watching what goes on in the barnyard and coming to their own conclusions about how all that applies to their own private parts. The problem now is that most Americans no longer live on farms or even near them, so what we're left with for sexual instructors are a few domestic pets like dogs and cats and goldfish.

As far as cats go, you're unlikely to see much of anything involving sexual matters. They do their business in the night with so much scratching and screeching that it makes sex sound about as appealing as being locked in a room with a manicurist who files fingernails on a chalkboard. In fact, a cat is so private about its sex life that you'll be lucky if you can even determine what gender the darn thing is. If it'll let you raise its tail, you may notice what looks like a punctuation mark under there. An upside-down semicolon means it's a female; a colon means it's a male. But if you flunked English, that won't help you explain matters to your parents. You may want to turn to the dogs for further clarification.

Dogs (as you may have noticed from the way the neighbor's Pekingese has been rubbing your trousers) are a lot less discreet about their sex lives. Dogs are likely to do the deed at any time of day to any kind of thing. The most unlikely pairing on record supposedly took place in South Wales back in the 1970s, when a male dachshund snuck up on a female Great Dane, who was sleeping at the time, and did IT (which we'll explain in more detail later) to her. What resulted was a baker's dozen of deformed dogs: Great Dachshunds that were never meant to be, with short little legs, enormous heads, and ears on end. It would have been enough to make your parents scratch their heads.

Come to think of it, you'd be better off taking a more forward approach. Try leaving some sexually informative material lying around where they'll see it — something like, say, a few good . . .

Dirty Books

There's no telling how many parents got their first inkling about sex back in the 1950s by reading the racy parts of *Peyton Place.* But one in six Americans did read Grace Metalious's novel, and certainly a few gleaned something from the heaving breasts and naked moonlit swims. For those (again) who weren't good at English, there was always the movie version, or the movie sequel, or the television series, or the television series sequel. But it was perhaps most titillating to have bought one of the 20 million copies knowing that the book had been banned in places like Canada, Rhode Island, and Fort Wayne,

175

A Visit from the Gods

In 1890, a statue of Apollo, commissioned sight unseen for an Ada, Ohio, college, arrived for its unveiling. When the sheet was lifted, wild screams filled the air, fleeing females disappeared in all directions, and there alone, in the center of the chaos, stood the cause of it all: the naked Apollo. Not until the statue had been properly clothed in velvet knee breeches did the women allow themselves to gaze upon it.

Indiana. If your parents were too embarrassed to buy *Peyton Place* themselves, you might have had trouble purchasing it for them, since fines were slapped on bookstore owners who sold it to underage customers.

Forbidden books, however gotten, have always helped get people interested in what they would otherwise overlook. Word of birth control, for instance, got passed around like a case of the clap in Boston (of all places) back in 1832, because the first published advice on the subject was banned outright. An otherwise harmless-looking pamphlet called *The Fruits of Philosophy: The Private Companion of Young Married People* should have been a sleeper but instead sold a quarter million copies.

Still, you say, your parents don't care about that. If their eyes glaze over when you quote to them from certain sexy books, you may have more luck letting them come upon a particular passage for themselves. Try opening a book to the most stimulating part and placing it where they'll be sure to see it. This is worth a shot, but don't get your hopes up too high. Mothers have been known simply to dust the book and put it back on the shelf.

At best you can conclude that although your mother doesn't fully appreciate dirty books, she can at least recognize a little good dirt. You may find it easier to give her (and your father) the education they need by simply sending them to college. College, of course, costs lots of money, but, what the heck, they'll learn many things there that *you* won't have to teach them. Things they should know and see, things like . . .

The Anatomy of Naked Bodies

In the Victorian period, when husbands would vacate a room if their wives so much as changed stockings, the idea of viewing a *whole* naked lady, even in a painting, was simply outrageous. Just the color of flesh tones in a portrait was considered indecent. What made art attractive back then was lots and lots of clothing.

Given that, you can *imagine* the inhibitions your parents have inherited (even if a *few* generations came between Victoria and them) and why it took someone as bland as Alfred Kinsey to shed some light on the subject of sex in 1938. Kinsey, at the time, was a professor of zoology best known for his collection of gall wasps at Indiana University. At his students' request, Kinsey went to research sex (at the library, not at home) and found that there wasn't much written. He followed up with more interviews. The report that resulted shocked the nation. It revealed, among other things, that masturbation did not cause mental illness; that more men and women engaged in premarital sex and extramarital sex than anyone had thought; and that healthy sex lives led to healthy marriages. There was still more to learn, and Kinsey's wife, Clara, said, "I hardly see him at night anymore since he took up sex."

Some critics compared the report to "the work of small boys writing dirty words on fences." Had it actually been graffiti, your parents might have read it. People tend to learn about sex in raunchier ways — by reading bathroom walls or playing spin the bottle, or doctor, or Barbie dolls (with Ken in the camper), or some such thing.

The teachers in sixth-grade sex ed class try their best to sanitize it by projecting diagrams of the human body on the wall, but of course those make no sense. In his sex book, James Thurber jokingly supplants an anatomy diagram with a chart of the North Atlantic depicting airplane routes. "The authors realize that this will be of no help to the sex novice," Thurber writes, "but neither is a cross section of the human body."

Ken: "Hey, Doll, how about a ride in the camper?"
Barbie: "No Ken do."

When it comes right down to it, visual aids will do little to keep your parents' attention. What you'll finally have to resort to is simply shoveling the information at them as fast as you can in hopes that when they get a little older, they'll understand.

The simplest explanation you can give about where babies come from is, of course, . . .

The Stork Theory

It was the Scandinavians who first concocted the story of the stork arriving with the swaddled baby in its beak. The stork was the perfect bird for the job — it was caring, gentle, monogamous. Naturalists have noted that storks, who live up to 70 years, return annually to nest on the same chimney stack and offer great care to their young and old alike. In fact, your parents will be happy to know that the stork goes so far as to offer an extended wing of support for an aged parent and, because of that, the ancient Romans passed "The Stork's Law," requiring offspring to care for their elderly folks.

The very word *stork* comes from the Greek word *storge,* meaning "strong and natural affection." So it all makes sense: this kind, sweet bird brings Mommy a cute little baby, and Mommy has nothing more to do than take it in her arms. So why, then, is the mother always stuck in bed after the baby's arrival? Well that, legend says, is because the nice bird bit Mommy's leg on the way out the door.

You'll note from that last little twist that you are allowed to extrapolate on these legends to make them suit your purposes. If you are extremely bright, you can even turn birth legends to enormous profit. Take, for instance, the guy who not only appropriated the tale that babies are found in . . .

The Cabbage Patch

. . . but then proceeded to sell them as dolls. That man was Georgia sculptor Xavier Roberts, who back in 1983, you'll recall, came up with a magnificent marketing ploy for some chubby-cheeked dolls. Instead of merely selling the dolls made in his art gallery, he put them up for "adoption" from "Babyland General Hospital," where salesclerks dressed as doctors and nurses lifted them from incubators and bassinets.

The Stork Express: A fly-by-night delivery service.

"An oath of adoption" and a list of promises was required from each "adopter." People went nuts to get them. One desperate Kansas City postman flew all the way to London to "adopt" a Cabbage Patch Kid. Altogether that year, $60 million worth of Cabbage Patch dolls were sold. In the following years, the baby-making legend grew to include variations from Pumpkin Kids to Blossom Babies to Cauliflower Babies and, yes, even Garbage Pail Kids.

Garbage Pail Kids? Your parents might choke at the thought of babies blooming in the muck, but long ago that was the respectable explanation for procreation. In medieval times, it was said that life sprang out of pure and simple . . .

Coming soon to a cabbage patch near you . . .

Spontaneous Combustion

The theory went that flies and worms and assorted crawling creatures took form in warm, rotted slime. Careful experimentation had revealed that a woman's hair dropped in the water would produce a snake, and that wheat fermented in water for 21 days would make a mouse.

From there it was only natural that people would come up with all sorts of wild ideas about the births of all sorts of higher life forms (like us). In Queensland, they said that babies were formed from swamp mud by the thunder god, then stuck in the womb of a woman. Others said that a woman got pregnant by sitting over a fire where a certain fish had been roasted. An eastern Australian tribe said that baby girls

179

Sex Training

Certain athletes could enhance their physical performances on the field by having sex the night before a big game, says psychology professor Susan Butt of the University of British Columbia. Butt, Canada's top-ranked female tennis player in the 1960s, came to that conclusion after studying more than 70 references ranging from Sigmund Freud to Masters and Johnson. She found that the same rule about overtraining (i.e., don't overdo it) should apply to sex and that sex as a form of exercise can keep athletes healthy and living longer.

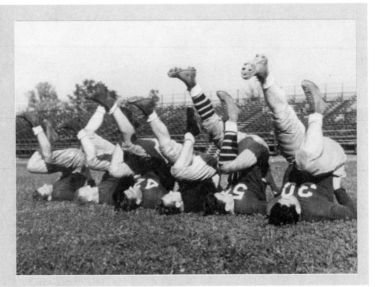

were made by the moon and baby boys by the wood lizard. Perhaps most improbable of all was the legend of another Australian tribe, which claimed that a woman conceived when a man she wasn't married to sent the spirit of a dying kangaroo her way.

As for what determined the baby's gender, the ancient Greeks believed that males came from the left side of the womb and females from the right. Aristotle said that a boy would come if the north wind blew and a girl would come from the south wind. So you see, even the great philosophers of ancient times had trouble with the concepts. They came up with all sorts of imaginative things, such as . . .

The Chinese Puzzle Box Theory

This one, which was going around during the last quarter of the 17th century, was better known as "The Encasement Theory." The idea was that Eve's ova were packaged like a Chinese puzzle box, with all the future generations of eggs coming out of it over time, leaving one less ovum for each generation, until after 200 million generations, all the ova would run out, ending humankind as we know (and love) it. But then microscopes came along, and people looked at sperm close up and saw *(Can you believe it?! Harold, come look at this!)* a whole human face and a little huddled body with legs and arms all there in the head of the sperm. From there they extrapolated that Adam's sperm must have contained a homunculus (a little man) packaged like a Russian doll, with all the future generations' sperm inside that first one.

None of those ideas turned out to be accurate after all. Babies don't come gift-wrapped exclusively in either the man's sperm or the woman's egg. It takes, as we know now, the combination of both of them to form a new life. To clarify exactly how the egg and sperm get joined, we think it is time you sat your parents down and told them all about . . .

The Birds & the Bees

We must caution here that although the birds and the bees analogy has been the most commonly used in explaining sex, it also has been the most mystifying. On careful study, you will notice that birds and bees have absolutely nothing in common with people as far as sex is concerned.

In fact, a whole colony of bees is basically sexless. Only one female and one male out of *thousands* has even the *slightest* chance for a one-time, fly-by-night interlude. Then it's over. The males are kicked out to die. The queen bee is left as a baby-making blimp in a dark room. What your parents can learn from all that is not readily apparent.

As for birds, they are only slightly better for instructive purposes. They allow a glimpse of a couple caring for an egg, it's true, and they do get extra points for monogamy, but as for the sexual details of their union, there really isn't much to see. The guy bird, we are sorry to say, in most species does not have the expected apparatus. What he's got is a cloaca — a sort of hacked-off vacuum cleaner hose that sucks up to *her* hacked-off vacuum cleaner hose so that . . .

Oh, no . . . now we've done it. We've mentioned the unspeakable — dirt and vacuum cleaners — and your mother is off cleaning again. It seems we've said enough for now. When she gets older, she'll understand. ♥

The birds and the bees: Don't get it? You're not alone.

Yes, Virginia, There Really Is an Aphrodisiac That Works

Bat blood? Crocodile dung?

Hippopotamus snout? Well, maybe not . . .

It is a delicate matter. One, perhaps, you'd rather not discuss. We understand. We all get tired, all find ourselves now and then lacking the *thrust* of excitement we once had upon preparing for bed. You know those nights. (Just how many headaches can you *have* in one week?) Face it, you could use a little help, a little stimulation.

Suppose you had just what the doctor ordered — a dose of bear gallbladder, a dusting of Spanish fly — that would result in the erotic experience of your life, peak ecstasy over and over? Would you give $20,000 for an ounce of potent love potion? Would you descend into a cave of tarantulas and snakes and bird guano for an absolutely amazing aphrodisiac? Would you risk disease? Death? Dismemberment? Be honest. You might, just once, to see what you've been missing.

You are not alone. People from the most ordinary

Which is more effective: hyena eyes or hippopotamus snout? For centuries, the question has stirred men and women to further research.

This Is Your Life, Casanova

Most people have heard that the young Casanova was the greatest adventurer and lover of his time, but not many know what became of him. In his later years, he lived in Bohemia and worked for Count von Waldstein in the Chateau de Dux as — of all things — a librarian. The renowned lover passed away quietly in the stacks, leaving many women disappointed, no doubt, and many men relieved.

places have tried the most extraordinary stimulants: powder from the horns of rhinos, ground heel bones from the Austrian Alpine ibex, snake bile laced with kaolin, bat blood mixed with whiskey. And wait, there's more! Crocodile dung. Shark fin soup. Bird's-nest soup. Turtle eggs. Seal penises. Siberian tiger penises. Deer penises steeped in rice wine with wolfberries (makes you drool). You get the idea: the more exotic, the more erotic. If it's hard to get, it must be good.

And if it's good, it must cost lots. You want a pair of Alaskan walrus tusks? That'll cost you $8,000. An ounce of bear gallbladder? Hand over $10,000. A rhino horn? Twenty thousand. On the cheap end, we can get you a little Chattanooga beluga — that bluish gray caviar from freshwater paddlefish — for $500 a pound. After you've spent enough dough, you'll be sure to stay awake to get your money's worth. Whatever happens, you're *bound* to find it memorable.

The downside to this exotic aphrodisiac business is that rare species are being decimated. "Our wildlife is under siege," the director of the U.S. Fish and Wildlife Service recently told *Newsweek*. Officials have estimated the trade in illegal animal parts at around $2.1 billion a year — up nearly 100 percent from a decade ago. The whole business is now second only to the global drug trade in illegal profits.

Money and moral issues aside, the big question is this: Do aphrodisiacs really work? Hope is a great stimulant, and people have hoped for sexual euphoria since ancient times. The very word *aphrodisiac* goes all the way back to the Greek goddess of love — that queen of beauty and sensuality, Aphrodite. She has inspired cultures throughout the ages to try to achieve her legendary heights of delight.

In 1400 B.C., one of the first great Hindu physicians, Susruta, recommended that impotent Hindus consume animal testicles to raise their testosterone levels. Pliny the Elder recommended hippopotamus snout and hyena eyes, while Horace touted dried marrow and liver. In Elizabethan times, prunes were so highly regarded as aphrodisiacs that they were served free in brothels. More dramatically, in 1889, a daring French physiologist named Charles-Édouard Brown-Séquard injected himself with a mixture of dog testicles, guinea pig testicles, and saline solution in the purely scientific interests of sexology. He was happy to report "a remarkable return of physical endurance." Five years later, he was, unfortunately, dead.

The Danger-Desire Connection

Although we can't be sure of the direct connection in that particular case, we can be sure the link between sex and danger exists in many other instances. Even the possibility of death has heightened love affairs throughout the ages. That erotic urgency has sparked countless wartime romances, tweaked endless spy thrillers, and charged numerous illicit affairs. The presence of danger, in fact, is its own aphrodisiac.

Scientists have tested the theory in their labs. One study, which we'll call "The Bridge Over Troubled Water Report," went like this: Researchers erected a suspension bridge, which presented a frightening challenge to the single men they asked to cross it. A subject made his heroic way over the swaying bridge and, halfway across, unexpectedly encountered a woman. In his heightened state of anxiety, the subject noted that her eyes were especially bright. The researchers recorded the response. The experiment was repeated with another unsuspecting gentleman. Then another, and so on.

Later, the scientists observed what happened when the same woman approached a single man in an office setting. In that case, the calm men looked up with no special interest. The scientists repeated the experiment: more men in suits, more apathy.

The results were tabulated, and — surprise! — the researchers concluded that a man who meets a woman in a precarious situation — on a trembling bridge, say — is more likely to remember her with heart a-

Sometimes danger can lead to desire. This fellow wouldn't fall for just anyone.

flutter and more likely to ask her out on a date. The office man will do nothing. Proof that danger ranks high as an aphrodisiac.

Putting Your Best Foot Forward

Proof number two comes from what we'll call "The Footsie Survey." Let's consider danger in the form of a secret affair. Psychologist Daniel Wegner at the University of Virginia tested the theory on 96 college students, pairing them with members of the opposite sex. He instructed all of them to take part in a game of cards (not by its nature a very stimulating exercise), then divided them into three groups. The couples in the first group could talk to each other but couldn't have any physical contact. The couples in the second group could communicate only nonverbally, by secretly playing footsie under the table. The couples in the third group could communicate by touching feet openly. None of the students knew each other beforehand.

The experiment began. The couples laid their proverbial cards on the table. When it was over, Wegner checked the chemistry between the partners. What he discovered was that those who simply talked to each other and those who touched feet openly were much less attracted to their partners than those who had been forced to conceal their foot caresses. The risk of detection had indeed heightened their erotic feelings for one another.

A little chocolate could sweeten things up.

Secrecy gets the juices flowing, but so does the brain chemical phenylethylamine. The same PEA that the brain releases during the early stages of infatuation — the revver-upper that allows us to stay awake all night and makes us lose our appetites — is also what races through the system of the thrill seeker. By raising the blood pressure and sending the heart racing, PEA allows the adventurer to feel alert, self-assured, and ready for whatever challenge awaits him or her. That thrill can come from love or conquest — or chocolate. Chocolate, many believe, is the love drug — that luscious and indulgent melting in the mouth that makes amphetamines spurt and stirs up all sorts of sexy feelings. The Mexican emperor Montezuma considered it such a virility booster that he drank 50 cups of chocolate a day before visiting his harem of 600 women. But despite its sensual appeal and PEA content, the true effect of chocolate on the libido is still scientifically debated. When taken in large quantities, chocolate may even have a negative effect on sexual prowess, reports Dr. Wayne Meikle of the University of Utah. He found that men who consumed too much high-fat food had a 30 percent drop in testosterone level.

Speaking of testosterone, modern research has shown, in a surprising twist, that testosterone has a more remarkable effect on older women than on older men. Small doses of testosterone prescribed to post-menopausal women by psychologist Barbara Sherwin at McGill University dramatically increased the women's sexual desire and energy levels. It was so effective, in fact, that some husbands whined about their wives' "overcharged" sex drive.

Bedroom Habits of the Rich & Famous

If you've ever wondered what secret things famous people have done between the sheets, we can now reveal these startling facts: Mark Twain, F. Scott Fitzgerald, and Edith Wharton all . . . wrote in bed. The legendary sex queen Mae West, known especially for her bedroom skills, went even further. She completed not only several screenplays in bed but her autobiography as well. "Everybody knows I do my best work in bed," she forthrightly said.

For those guys with flagging libidos, we offer a few tips from the great romantics of the past and present. Casanova championed oysters; Napoleon treasured truffles; Popeye performed manly feats on a can of spinach; the maharajah of Bikaner ingested crushed diamonds (though we haven't the strong stomach or great fortunes to recommend it ourselves); some professional basketball players swear by ginseng; certain celebrity bodybuilders praise Hot Stuff (a protein powder of yohimbe bark, from an African tree, which veterinarians use for bull breeding and which can be lethal in humans in high doses).

To be perfectly honest, the U.S. Food and Drug Administration (FDA) has declared all sex drugs lame. In 1989, they banned advertisers from

"Every plant bears some mark of the use to which it can be put..."

promoting rooster pills or potions, because their testing had shown that none worked no matter what the content — fennel or strychnine or dried beetle bodies. The FDA said that the love potions were only placebos. Any that appeared to work did so only because the user *believed* they would. The stimulant lay only in the user's mind.

When Passion Goes to Your Head

In other words, it is the imagination that creates its own exciting possibilities and the body that leaps forward to fulfill the fantasies. Perhaps that's why a recent survey by the University of Chicago's National Opinion Research Center showed that of all possible sexual activities, Americans' second favorite was watching their mates undress. The anticipation, it seems, is almost as sweet as the culmination.

And anticipation often begins with food. In more than 500 literary seduction scenes, the *Aphrodisiac Growers Quarterly* reported, 98 percent begin with a succulent meal. The list of foods thought to stir passion is long and seemingly random. But chances are the food is considered an aphrodisiac for one or more of the following four reasons.

First, because of its sensuous, fleshy texture and taste of the sea (oysters, mussels, caviar, herring, lobster, that sort of thing). Second, because the food (such as asparagus, carrots, mandrake root, ginseng root, and lupines) grows in the shape of the male sex organ and therefore falls within the Doctrine of Signs — "that every plant bears some mark of the use to which it can be put."

Third, because the food acts as a sort of sexual smelling salt (think of chili peppers, garlic, and onions) that tingles the tongue and makes the nostrils flare.

Fourth, because it's a natural rejuvenator — an herb with properties that enhance vigor and vitality or supply missing minerals. In the words of the Kamasutra, "A man should eat strengthening foods, such as aromatic plants, meat, honey and eggs. A robust constitution is indispensable." A man lacking zinc is a man lacking a high sperm count. Feed him oysters rich in zinc, or asparagus, or the dark meat of a turkey.

Just beware that you don't overdo it with any one food. In the words of Dr. Frederick Hollick, a roving medical expert in the 1840s, "In all cases, avoid constipation, the hand maiden of impotence and derangement." And further, be advised, as Dr. Hollick noted, that "sexual indulgence just after eating is nearly certain to be followed by indigestion, even if it does not cause immediate vomiting."

The Last Stimulant You'll Ever Need

What you are aiming for is well-moderated, plain and simple good health. Take it from the Kinsey Institute for the Study of Human Sexuality, which advocates not only a good diet but also plenty of rest and regular exercise to keep the circulation pumping. When the body feels fit, the impulse to procreate will follow.

Beyond the body, there is only the mind. If you are a man who is still lacking in oomph, go forth and make yourself rich or powerful or the caretaker of a baby. For there are women who say that money is the true aphrodisiac, that power is sexy, that there is nothing more alluring than a man holding a baby. In the end, arousal has the most to do with believing that a particular man will fulfill your fantasies not only in the bedroom but beyond — by offering diamonds or fame or the perfect father for your kids.

The final stimulant is love, the most magnificent of aphrodisiacs. If properly applied, love can raise sexual intimacy to a height more explosive and enduring than could ever be reached through any amount of rhinoceros powder. And although love is certainly no easier to get hold of, it is a heck of a lot cheaper and more environmentally correct. ♥

A little love will do what all the rhino horns in the world can't manage.

189

Forever After

When

all is said and done, it will be up to you and your spouse alone to find your way from here to eternity. Any couple that manages to do so has managed to stake out a claim on the mountain of immortality, for they are sure to live forever in each other's eyes and in the hearts of all those who look to them for inspiration. We offer here a few stories in that vein. The story of the breakfast tray that fed a couple's love; the story of the man who tried to pull his wife over a barn roof; the story of a wife who took smug satisfaction in giving her husband the last word. But before you begin all that, take a minute for our marriage IQ test — and see just how much you really know about the subject.

Test Your Marriage IQ

*Get out your pencils, sharpen your wit —
this is the test you've all been waiting for.
It's time to prove to your spouse that you
know more than she (no, he) does . . .*

To become a doctor or a lawyer, you have to study for years and pass all sorts of exams. To get a marriage license, in many states you need only pass a blood test (no late-night studying required). But once you're hitched, you are (theoretically) committed for life, and a change of spouse won't come as easily as a change of career might. You are committed to making this marriage work, and it'd be a lot easier to do if you didn't become disconsolate like the couple in the encyclopedia ad: "One year married and all talked out." What you and your spouse are shooting for is stellar conversation. And what the ad offers as stimulus is a set of Harvard Classics. "If they would only buy the Five-Foot Shelf and study it fifteen minutes a day, they might turn their silent, lonely hours into real human companionship." To save you the expense of a full set of encyclopedias, we offer you here (free of charge!) a few openers for those days when you find yourself suffering from a rather rare but particularly dull moment in your married life.

If the thrill has gone from your marriage, it may be time to put you and your spouse to the test.

193

1. Two hundred years ago, scientists believed that you could decipher the mysteries of a person's affections by studying the location of moles on his or her body. According to their theory, what does a mole on your nose signify?
   a. That you will marry fast, and often, and will parent many children.
   b. That you will cheat on your spouse.
   c. That you will demonstrate a keen ability to sniff out indiscretion.
   d. That your spouse will insist you have facial surgery.

2. The great Irish novelist and poet James Joyce was nicknamed which of the following by his wife?
   a. My Little Gummy Bear.
   b. Big Jim.
   c. Simpleminded Jim.
   d. The Wordmeister.

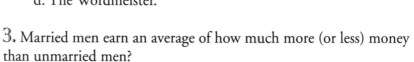

What wa[s] Nora's r[…] nicknam[e] for Joyc[e]

3. Married men earn an average of how much more (or less) money than unmarried men?
   a. 31 percent less.
   b. 31 percent more.
   c. 10 percent more.
   d. Roughly the same.

4. According to *The Folklore of Weddings and Marriage*, a mother-in-law can test her new daughter-in-law's housewifery skills by doing which of the following?
   a. Examining a sample of her daughter-in-law's writing for crossed t's and dotted i's.
   b. Placing a broom on the floor.
   c. Inspecting her son's shirt collars for stains.
   d. Placing a pea under her daughter-in-law's mattress.

So fur, so good: A ruffled tabby means what?

194

5. What American president was the only president to wed in the White House? (Hint: He was 48; she was 21. They married in 1886 and were entertained at their wedding by John Philip Sousa and the Marine Corps Band.)

6. The fur of a cat blowing the wrong way means what about your husband's habits?

    a. He was ruffled by something you said last night and wishes you would ask him about it so that he can get it off his chest and not be forced to go and tell his mother that you're a slouch.

    b. He's a clumsy shaver.

    c. He likes his eggs runny.

    d. He's looking favorably at another woman.

7. During the Victorian age, which of the following topics were spouses *not* allowed to speak to each other about?

    a. Birth control, hygiene, underclothes, sex.

    b. Illness, insanity, illegitimate children.

    c. Physiology, prostitution, suicide, homosexuality.

    d. All of the above.

8. The Annual Study of Women's Attitudes found in 1987 that 87 percent of women in the United States believe that extramarital sex is *not* acceptable. So what's the likelihood that an American woman will *have* an extramarital affair (according to the Institute for Social Research)?

    a. 5 percent.

    b. 13 percent.

    c. 25 percent.

    d. 40 percent.

9. What great Egyptian beauty was married to her own brother?

10. Who was the only American president never to marry?

In Love with an Old Funny Bone

A good sense of humor is sure to take two spouses a long way into marriage. A respect for the aging process will take them from there. Agatha Christie combined both in a delightful way when she wrote, "An archaeologist is the best husband a woman can have; the older she gets, the more interested he is in her."

Luckily for Christie, she was married to one.

195

11. Who was the first sitting governor to marry a member of Congress?

12. According to a recent study by sociologists at the University of Washington, 45 percent of couples who had been married 2 years or less had sex 3 times per week. After 10 years of marriage, what percentage of couples continued to have sex 3 times per week?
    a. 45 percent.
    b. 18 percent.
    c. 5 percent.
    d. None.

13. During her lifetime, a woman is technically capable of giving birth up to about 25 times (though few would want to). Allowing for multiple births, what is the record number of babies ever delivered by one woman? (No, we're not talking about the doctor who *manages* the delivery.)
    a. 25.
    b. 32.
    c. 40.
    d. 69.

14. What percentage of American fathers are in the delivery room when their children are born?
    a. 29 percent.
    b. 56 percent.
    c. 60 percent.
    d. 79 percent.

15. What body chemical becomes most prevalent the longer a couple has been married?
    a. PEA.
    b. Aspirin.
    c. Endorphins.
    d. Alcohol.

16. What did Catherine the Great, empress of Russia, affectionately call the potbellied Grigori Potemkin?
    a. My Marble Beauty.
    b. Golden Rooster.
    c. Wolfbird.
    d. All of the above.

What the Dickens would he call her? Kate had great expectations.

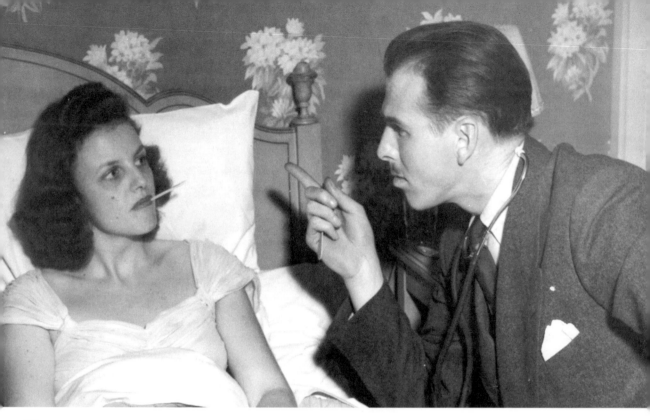

17. A divorced, middle-aged American woman stays sick in bed an average of two weeks per year. How much time does her married counterpart stay sick in bed per year?

Sick in bed or just sick of your marriage?

    a. None — she doesn't have time to get sick.
    b. Twice as long — in an effort to recover from the strain.
    c. The same amount of time.
    d. Only half as long.

18. In Charles Dickens's letters to his wife, Kate, he often gushed over her, using which of the following endearments?

    a. Dearest Mouse and Dearest, Darling Pig.
    b. Katie, oh Katie.
    c. My Dearest Dickens of a Dear.
    d. My Little Wifey.

19. What impassioned lover divorced the beautiful woman he adored to marry a stout, plain girl for whom he never cared?

20. A certain Pre-Raphaelite painter wrote a number of inspired love poems to his wife and, after her death, placed the verses in her hands and had them buried in her coffin. Seven and a half years later, he or-

> ☞ **From The** ☜
> **Old Farmer's Almanac**
>
> Make up your beds early in the morning; sew buttons on your husbands' shirts; do not rake up any grievances; protect the young and tender branches of your family; plant a smile of good temper on your face, root out all angry feelings, and expect a good crop of happiness.
>
> **—1862**

dered her body exhumed and the poems published. What was the rude romantic's name?

21. In Puritan New England, children born out of wedlock were how common?
- a. Nonexistent.
- b. Practically unheard-of.
- c. Somewhat common.
- d. All over the place.

22. Historically, among the Cashinahua Indians of Brazil, how did a man and a woman get married?
- a. In an open-air church with drums beating.
- b. By sleeping in a hammock together for a year.
- c. By stomping in unison 100 times around a circle.
- d. By eloping to Canada.

Broom as bride tester: a sweeping generalization.

He: "Would you care, my dear, to discuss the weather of today, of yesterday, or of the future?" She: "Not tonight, dear; I have a headache."

Answers

1. a. According to a compendium of pre-Freudian analysis called *A New Academy of Compliments,* published in 1795, "a mole on the nose signifies speedy and often marriages, and that the party will be fruitful in children." Whereas a mole on or near the private parts indicates that a person shows ability in duty, vigorousness in love, and success in raising many children.

2. c. Although James Joyce and Nora Barnacle were happily married, Nora disdained her husband's writing and would never have believed her "Simpleminded Jim" would come to be considered one of English literature's most brilliant stars.

Cleveland's wedding: a presidential first.

3. b. See, it pays to be married.

4. b. If the bride picks up the broom and sets it to one side, she will be a good housewife. If she steps over it, she will be a slouch.

5. Grover Cleveland married Frances Folsom — the girl who had been his ward since she was 12.

6. d. This situation, according to *The Folklore of Weddings and Marriage,* may be counteracted by greasing the cat's fur.

7. d. Victorian spouses were forced to keep their conversation to polite, discreet topics, like the day's weather, the previous day's weather, and the next day's weather. It's a wonder babies were born at all.

8. d. Go figure.

Catherine's drives were, well, Great.

9. Cleopatra VII could have married anyone she wanted, but she chose to marry her brother Ptolemy.

10. James Buchanan. His niece, Harriet Lane, acted as first lady.

11. Governor John McKernan married Representative Olympia Snowe on February 24, 1989. They had begun their courtship in 1979, when the two of them were the only U.S. representatives from Maine. At that time, it could be said that Maine's entire congressional delegation was dating each other. When they'd fly home to Maine from Washington for the weekend, they'd joke, "Your district or mine?"

12. b. But don't despair — quality is better than quantity. According to the Janus Report, three-fifths of married people found sex improved after marriage.

13. d. The Guinness record is held by a Russian woman who had 69 babies — mostly multiple births — during the course of 27 pregnancies (though it's hard to imagine).

14. d. We're happy to report that dads are more involved in births than ever.

15. c. After the chaotic infatuation of early love wears off, the morphinelike effect of endorphins takes over in the brain, creating a feeling of security and belonging. The other person's presence triggers the brain into a calming sort of trance, so that the longer a couple has been married, the longer they are likely to stay married in a happily "drugged" state.

16. d. Catherine, a woman of intense sexual appetites, had many pet names for her boorish lover.

17. d. Married women spend half as much time sick in bed. Marriage, you see, has all sorts of benefits.

18. a. Marital affection is a strange and wondrous thing.

◄ From The ►
Old Farmer's Almanac

"Harry!"
    "What is it, Dorothy?"
    "Did you give me that parlor lamp last Christmas, or did I give it to you?"

— 1907

19. Napoleon divorced Josephine for reasons of state (in other words, in hopes of producing an heir) and married Marie-Louise, daughter of the emperor of Austria.

20. Dante Gabriel Rossetti, whose *Poems* (the ones that were buried with his wife, Elizabeth Siddal) brought him greater fame than his paintings.

21. c. When the population of Boston stood at 4,000, there were 48 recorded cases of "bastardy" and 50 of fornication — a notable percentage during a time people usually associate with the more restrictive standards of Hawthorne's *Scarlet Letter.*

22. b. With the permission of her father, a teenage girl could ask a man she'd like to marry to sleep with her in her hammock. The suitor would arrive after the family had gone to sleep and leave before they awoke. If all went well, he would gradually bring his things to the family's house. After a year had passed, or after she had become pregnant, their marriage was considered a fait accompli.

How to Score Your Marriage IQ

If you got 22 answers right: You *must* have cheated, and we all know *that* doesn't work in marriage. Please try harder.

If you got 15–21 answers right: Congratulations! You know a heck of a lot of marriage trivia — which doesn't necessarily mean you're good at your own marriage, just that you have plenty to talk about at cocktail parties.

If you got 6–14 answers right: Maybe those Five-Foot Shelf encyclopedias aren't such a bad idea after all.

If you got 0–5 answers right: Well, hey, you're probably great at other things — like, say, mowing the lawn. It was nice of you even to bother. ♥

Can't cut it on the quiz? Better luck on the lawn.

10 Steps to a Happy Marriage

Start with an old coffeepot, a pine cone, and a pair of earrings . . .

1. For friendly relations between the bride and her mother-in-law, the mother-in-law should break a loaf of bread or cake over the daughter-in-law's head as she enters her new home. (Yes, this is good.)

2. Borrow a beat-up coffeepot for the first month or two of your marriage. Bringing a new coffeepot home is bad luck for the marriage.

3. Never let a man (even your husband) see you undress. If one does, it is certain to cause trouble in the family — and may lead to divorce.

4. If your husband should storm out of the house in a foul temper, go to a friend's house and eat applesauce. When your spouse arrives home, he will have forgotten his bad feelings.

Borrow an old coffeepot to perk things up; it keeps marriage from becoming a grind.

Expect trouble and distress if you see your spouse undress.

Catch and kiss an angry wife and you'll ensure domestic bliss. Or get your eyes gouged out — we forget which.

Bringing Home the Bacon

Being happily married in England in the 12th century was as good as winning the lottery. The husband and wife in each county who could prove that they had been the most joyously devoted to each other would win a side of cured and salted bacon. Oddly enough, the winners were selected by a jury of six bachelors and six unmarried women. The jurors quizzed the contestants on all manner of domestic issues and selected the happiest-sounding pair from amid the responses. The lucky newlyweds literally took home the bacon. Although the contest ended in the late 19th century, the phrase has continued in use.

[From The]
Old Farmer's Almanac

If things go wrong in the household, and the bread is heavy, do not make it heavier by fretting and finding fault. Cheerful and encouraging words will make digestion easier.

— 1896

5. If your wife becomes angry and tries to fight you, catch and kiss her while she is upset. If you do not, some other man will kiss her before the year is out.

6. If a husband should lose his temper, he must remove his hat and turn it around. Such action will bring immediate peace to the family. (This works only if he wears a hat, of course, so if he doesn't, best go buy him one fast.)

7. Put a pine cone under your pillow to ensure your husband's fidelity. (The stiff neck will be worth it.)

8. To prevent your wife from committing infidelity during your absence, place two halves of an acorn in her pillow.

9. Offer a deceived spouse a mild concoction of powdered mandrake root, which will provide a night of oblivion.

10. Buy a matched pair of earrings. Give one to your husband and keep the other for yourself. No matter how far you must be parted, sailors' legend says, you will always reunite. ♥

A spin of the hat can head off trouble.

205

"Till Death Do Us Part"

In the end, it is said, the only thing more enduring than death is love.

The French revolutionary Camille Desmoulins, friend of Robespierre's, wrote the following letter to his wife, Madame Lucile Desmoulins, at five o'clock on April 1, 1794. Despite his wife's struggle to save him, Camille was executed the morning after he penned these words.

When one sleeps, one has not the feeling of being in prison, one is free. Heaven had mercy on me. Only a moment ago, I saw you in my dream, I embraced you. . . . Our little one had lost an eye and I saw it in a bandage. And in my distress at this, I woke up. I found myself in my dungeon. Day was dawning. I saw you no more, my Lolotte, and could not hear you. . . . Oh, these cruel ones, who deprive me of the joy to hear these words, to see you and to make you happy. For that was my only ambition. . . .

Farewell, my precious Lucile, my Lolotte . . . my last moments shall not dishonour you. I was the husband of a woman of divine virtue, I was a good husband, a good son, I would also have been a good father. . . . My beloved Lucile, I was born to make verses and to defend the unfortunate. . . . I was born in order to make you happy, in order to create for us both, with your mother and my father and some intimate friends, a Tahiti. I dreamed the dreams of the Abbé Saint-Pierre. I dreamed of a republic, the idol of all men; I could not believe that men are so unjust and so cruel. . . .

Pardon me, my dear one, my true life, that I lost when we were separated, for occupying myself with memory. I had far better busy myself in making you forget. My Lucile, my dear Louploup, my darling, I implore you, do not call upon me; your cries will rend my heart even at the bottom of my grave. Care for your little one; live for my Horace; speak to him of me. Tell him hereafter what he cannot understand, that I should have loved him well. Notwithstanding my punishment, I believe there is a God. My blood will wash out my faults, my human weakness, and for the good I have done, for my virtues, my love of Liberty, God will reward me. I shall see you again one day. O Lucile! . . .

Good-bye, Louploup, my life, my soul, my heaven on earth! I leave you to good friends — all the sensible and virtuous men who remain. Good-bye — Lucile, my Lucile, my dear Lucile. . . . The shores of life recede from me. I see you still, Lucile, my beloved. My bound hands embrace you, and my head as it falls rests its dying eyes upon you.

Lucile Desmoulins was guillotined two weeks later. ♥

Camille Desmoulins wrote of a love that would endure forever.

How to Stay Married Forever

For those glum days when you wonder how the two of you

will ever work it out, we offer a little inspiration.

I. Tugging at the Heart of It

In 1770, Samuel Forbes was building a house on the Blackberry River in Canaan, Connecticut. During that time, he fell in love with a young woman named Lucy Peirce. It was a good match, for she equaled him in physique and strength of will. She also loved him. One night the two rode off to New York State — as the story goes, on the same unhappy horse — and were married.

When they arrived back home in Connecticut, Samuel took a long rope and threw one end over the barn.

"Now, my sweet," he reportedly said to his bride, "do you draw down

The couple that pulls together carries weight.

It Could Be Worse

On the days you feel you've married the wrong man, just remember, it could be worse. You could have married Henry VIII, who divorced his first wife, Catherine of Aragon, and beheaded his second, Anne Boleyn. He watched his third wife, Jane Seymour, die in childbirth, and divorced his fourth wife, Anne of Cleves, the same year that he married her. His fifth wife, Catherine Howard, he beheaded. His sixth and final wife, Catherine Parr, he left to widowhood.

on your end and I will draw on mine, and whichever draws the other over the roof is to rule this roost."

They both tugged hard. Nothing happened.

"Now, my sweet," Samuel called, "do you come around on this side, and let us draw together."

Lucy complied. Together they pulled the rope over the barn.

"Let that be the way this house will be run," declared Samuel. And apparently it was.

II. How to Keep Him Guessing

In *Love Medicine,* Louise Erdrich tells the story of a husband who left a good-bye note to his wife under the sugar jar and walked out. The wife later read it but knew he'd be home for supper. She purposely slipped his note beneath the peppershaker.

Sure enough, he returned home not long after, sat

down at the table, and saw the note still folded up. He slipped it in his pocket before his wife came in carrying his dinner. All was as it had been.

Except for the fact that for the rest of his married life, the husband had the nagging suspicion that he'd left the note under the sugar jar, *not* the peppershaker. He couldn't, of course, ask. And his wife couldn't, of course, help taking smug satisfaction in knowing that she'd gotten back at him for trying to walk out on her.

III. Feeding the Flame of Love

Sometimes it's the little things that make a marriage work. For Marilyn Myers Slade, the little thing happened to be a breakfast tray her mother gave her. When she got it, Marilyn suggested to her husband that they take turns serving each other breakfast in bed.

"I hate crumbs in bed," her husband protested. But that Sunday morning, he was ready for his tray, sitting up eagerly in bed.

When it was his turn to bring the tray to her, Marilyn was delighted to find it festively set with fruit slices laid in geometric patterns. Later, he placed a garden-picked blossom on a grapefruit half. Before long, he had decorated with everything from amaryllis leaves to maple buds. In winter, indoor plants such as scented geraniums and rosemary brightened her tray. She told him she was impressed with his flair. He told her he was inspired by her cooking.

Then one Saturday, he put a daisy hat on a fat red strawberry, and she decided it was time to take up the challenge. How could she top his whimsical artistry?

On a winter morning, she awoke with a vision. She reached out the door for a handful of snow and shaped it into a miniature snowman. A tiny pine cone made the perfect hat. She stuck the little man in the freezer and made breakfast. What would he think of this? She delivered the tray to his bedside and quickly headed down the stairs. A whoop of laughter followed her out.

"You've won the prize," he said. "Yes, sir, you've won the prize!"

In marriage, a little creativity might snowball.

210

Honey, I've Got This Crazy Idea for a TV Show . . .

If Ozzie and Harriet were the icons of married life on television in the 1950s and 1960s, Lucy and Ricky Ricardo (Lucille Ball and Desi Arnaz) were the unexpected (and most hilarious) ones.

In real life, Lucy and Desi had to overcome the challenge of being pulled in two directions — he was drawn to nightclubs, while she was tied to Hollywood. Luckily, Lucy came up with the idea of a television show that would star them both as husband and wife. Skeptical CBS executives didn't think audiences would fall for a Latin musician married to a wild redhead, so Lucy and Desi put up their own money for the pilot. Sure enough, *I Love Lucy* hit it big. The highlight came in 1953 when the two made TV history. On that night, the real Lucy gave birth to Desi Arnaz IV in the hospital, while her televised self gave birth to Little Ricky on the air.

IV. Giving Him the Last Word

Every year the Boston Elderly Affairs Commission holds a Valentine's
Day dance for Boston couples who have been married at least half a
century. The 50 or so couples who attend the soiree can count some
2,600 married years among them.

To have that sort of success, you're bound to have a secret. Sure enough,
most do have advice for staying married. Although the wisdom isn't
always consistent, it's always enlightening in one way or another.

Some say don't leave the house if you get in an argument with a
spouse. Others say definitely go out for a walk. One man says simply
don't argue, don't smoke, and don't drink. While his wife adds the obvious — *don't* fool around.

But perhaps the best words of wisdom come from Anne Gilberto
of East Boston, who's been married to Steve for more than 50 years.
In that time, they've reached a form of compromise that not only gets
things done but also lets them both take satisfaction in having had
their own way. The secret to their long marriage, says Anne, is this:

"I always give him the last word. I tell him what to do, and he
says, 'Yes, ma'am.'" ♥

Top This

The longest two mar-
riages on record lasted
86 years each. One was
the marriage of cousins
Sir Temulji Bhicaji Na-
riman and Lady Nariman,
who wed in 1853 at age
five. The other marriage
of that length was be-
tween Lazarus Rowe of
Greenland, New Hamp-
shire, and Molly Webber.
Married in 1743, when
both were 18, they raised
a large family and lived to
see descendants of the
fifth generation. Imagine.

Credits

Text Credits

Grateful acknowledgment is made to the following for permission to reprint previously published material.

Sally Reeds: "The Honeymoon Suite That Wasn't," by Sally Reeds from the November 1993 issue of *Condé Nast Traveler*, first published as "Romantic Refund." Reprinted with permission of the author.

Schlesinger Library, Radcliffe College: "For the Love of Lydia," from the Lydia Marie Auerbach Parsons Papers, Schlesinger Library, Radcliffe College.

Picture Credits

An Introduction to Falling in Love. Pages 3, 4–5: Dover Publications, computer enhanced by Dave Nelson.

The Search. Pages 6–7: FPG International. Page 8: Dover Publications. Pages 8–9: National Gallery of Art, Washington, Widener Collection (Titian, *Venus and Adonis*). Page 10: Yankee Archives. Pages 11, 12: Dover Publications. Page 13 (top): H. Armstrong Roberts. Page 13 (bottom): Dover Publications. Pages 14–15: photograph by Vyto Starinskas, © Rutland *Daily Herald*, Rutland, Vermont. Page 16: Dave Nelson. Page 17: Dover Publications, computer enhanced by Dave Nelson. Page 19: H. Armstrong Roberts. Page 20: Dave Nelson. Pages 21, 22: Dover Publications. Pages 22–23: H. Armstrong Roberts. Page 24: Dover Publications. Page 25: FPG International. Page 26: H. Armstrong Roberts. Page 27: Courtesy, Museum of Fine Arts, Boston (Auguste Renoir, *Le Bal à Bougival*). Page 28: Yankee Archives. Page 29: FPG International. Pages 30, 31: Dover Publications.

The Kiss. Pages 32–33: FPG International. Page 34: Dave Nelson. Pages 34–35: Robert W. Young/FPG International. Page 35: Dover Publications, computer enhanced by Dave Nelson. Page 36: Louise Van Der Meid/FPG International. Pages 37, 38 (top): Dover Publications. Page 38 (bottom): Dave Nelson. Page 39: Yankee Archives. Page 40: FPG International. Page 41 (top): Camerique/H. Armstrong Roberts. Page 41 (bottom): Yankee Archives. Page 42: FPG International, computer enhanced by Dave Nelson. Page 43 (top): Photofest. Pages 43 (bottom), 44 (top): Dover Publications. Page 44 (bottom): Yankee Archives. Page 45: The Bettmann Archive. Page 46: Dover Publications. Page 47: FPG International. Pages 49, 50: Photofest. Page 51: Dover Publications. Pages 52–53: H. Armstrong Roberts. Pages 52–53 (inset): Photofest. Page 53: H. Armstrong Roberts. Page 54: Dover Publications. Page 55: Photofest.

The Courtship. Pages 56–57: H. Armstrong Roberts. Pages 58–59: Dover Publications. Page 60: Dave Nelson. Pages 61, 62–63: Yankee Archives. Pages 64–65: Archive Photos/Hirz. Page 66: Dover Publications. Page 67: H. Armstrong Roberts. Page 68: Dover Publications. Pages 70, 72: H. Armstrong Roberts. Page 73: Archive Photos. Page 75: H. Armstrong Roberts. Page 76: Dover Publications. Page 77: Paul Giambarba. Page 78: Yankee Archives. Page 79: Dover Publications. Page 80: Yankee Archives. Page 81: Photofest. Page 82: Archive Photos/American Stock. Pages 83, 84: Dover Publications. Page 85: from *Life*, December 6, 1900. Page 86: Yankee Archives. Page 88: Dover Publications. Page 89: The Bettmann Archive. Page 90: Yankee Archives. Page 91: Photofest. Page 92: H. Armstrong Roberts. Page 93: Dover Publications.

The Engagement. Pages 94–95: H. Armstrong Roberts. Page 96: Dover Publications. Pages 96–97: Photofest. Page 98: Yankee Archives. Page 99: Dover Publications. Page 100: FPG International. Page 101 (top): Dover Publications. Page 101 (bottom): Dover Publications, computer enhanced by Dave Nelson. Page 102: H. Armstrong Roberts. Page 103 (top): Dave Nelson. Page 103 (bottom): Dover Publications, computer enhanced by Dave Nelson. Page 104: Photofest. Page 105: Oregon Historical Society, neg. no. OrHi 36011. Pages 106–7: FPG International. Page 108: Dover Publications. Page 109: Yankee Archives. Page 110: Dover Publications. Pages 110–11, 112: H. Armstrong Roberts. Page 113: Photofest. Page 114: FPG International. Page 115: Dover Publications. Page 116: FPG International. Page 117: FPG International/Photoworld. Page 118: Dover Publications. Page 119: Courtesy, Department of Library Services, American Museum of Natural History (neg. No. 337696). Page 121: Dover Publications.

The Wedding. Pages 122–23: H. Armstrong Roberts. Pages 124–27: Illustration by Ron Barrett. Page 129: Photofest. Pages 130, 131: AP/Wide World. Page 132: Index Stock Photography/Black Box. Page 133: AP/Wide World. Pages 134–37: Matt Wawiorka. Page 138: Dover Publications. Page 139: Brown Brothers. Page 140: Dover Publications, computer enhanced by Dave Nelson. Page 141: Archive Photos.

The Honeymoon. Pages 142–43: H. Armstrong Roberts. Page 144: Dover Publications. Pages 144–45: H. Armstrong Roberts. Page 146: Archive Photos. Page 147: Dover Publications. Page 148 (left): Yankee Archives. Page 148 (right): H. Armstrong Roberts. Page 149: Archive Photos/American Stock. Pages 150–51: Photofest. Pages 152–53: Illustration © CSA Archive. Pages 154, 155: Dover Publications. Page 156: Photofest. Page 157: Dover Publications, computer enhanced by Dave Nelson. Page 158: The Bettmann Archive. Page 159: © Museum of the City of New York, The Harry T. Peters Collection. Pages 160–61: H. Armstrong Roberts. Page 162: from *A Book of New England Legends and Folk Lore* by Samuel Adams Drake, Boston, 1902.

Sex. Pages 164–65: Frauke/Mauritius/H. Armstrong Roberts. Page 166: Dover Publications, computer enhanced by Dave Nelson. Page 167 (top): Archive Photos. Page 167 (top, inset): Photofest. Page 167 (bottom): H. Armstrong Roberts. Pages 168, 169: Dover Publications, computer enhanced by Dave Nelson. Page 170: H. Armstrong Roberts. Page 171: Sarah Hale. Page 172: Dover Publications. Pages 172–73: H. Armstrong Roberts. Page 174: Sarah Hale. Page 175: Dover Publications. Page 176: Dover Publications, computer enhanced by Dave Nelson. Page 177: Archive Photos. Page 178: Dover Publications. Page 179: Yankee Archives. Page 180: Archive Photos/Lambert. Pages 181, 182: Dover Publications. Pages 182–83: Corbis-Bettmann. Page 184: Archive Photos/Camera Press. Pages 185, 186: H. Armstrong Roberts. Page 187: Photofest. Page 188: Courtesy, Dewitt Historical Society of Tompkins Co. (neg. no. N1, 1036). Page 189: Dover Publications.

Forever After. Pages 190–91: H. Armstrong Roberts. Page 192: Dover Publications. Pages 192–93: Archive Photos/Lambert. Page 194 (top): FPG International. Page 194 (bottom): Dover Publications. Page 195: FPG International. Page 196: Dover Publications. Page 197: FPG International. Page 198 (top and bottom): Dover Publications. Page 199: FPG International. Page 200: The Bettmann Archive. Pages 201, 202: Dover Publications. Pages 202–3, 204: Photofest. Page 205 (top): Dover Publications, computer enhanced by Dave Nelson. Page 205 (bottom): Dover Publications. Page 207: Corbis-Bettmann. Page 208: Dover Publications. Page 209 (top): H. Armstrong Roberts. Page 209 (bottom): Dave Nelson. Page 210: Illustration © CSA Archive. Page 211: Photofest. Page 212: Yankee Archives.

Note: Diligence was exercised in locating owners of all images used. If an image was uncredited or mistakenly credited, please contact the publisher and effort will be made to include credit in future printings.